COMMUNICATE!

A Communication Skills Guide
for Health Care Workers

Communicate!

A Communication Skills Guide
for Health Care Workers

Philip Burnard, PhD,

Director of Postgraduate Nursing Studies,
University of Wales College of Medicine,
Cardiff
and
Honourary Lecturer,
Hogeschool Midden Nederland,
Utrecht, Netherlands

Edward Arnold
A division of Hodder & Stoughton
LONDON MELBOURNE AUCKLAND

© 1992 Philip Burnard

First published in Great Britain 1992

British Library Cataloguing in Publication Data

Burnard, Philip
  Communicate!: A communication skills guide for health
  care workers.
  I. Title
  362.1023

  ISBN 0–340–55787–7

Whilst the advice and information in this book is believed to be true
and accurate at the date of going to press, neither the author nor the
publisher can accept any legal responsibility or liability for any errors
or omissions that may be made. In particular (but without limiting the
generality of the preceding disclaimer) every effort had been made to
check drug dosages; however, it is still possible that errors have been
missed. Furthermore, dosage schedules are constantly being revised
and new side effects recognised. For these reasons the reader is
strongly urged to consult the drug companies' printed instructions
before administering any of the drugs recommended in this book.

Typeset in Baskerville by Anneset, Weston-super-Mare, Avon.
Printed and bound in Great Britain for Edward Arnold, a division of
Hodder and Stoughton Limited, Mill Road, Dunton Green,
Sevenoaks, Kent TN13 2YA by Thomson Litho Ltd, East Kilbride,
Glasgow.

Other Books By
The Same Author

Learning Human Skills: An Experiential Guide for Health Professionals, 2nd edn.

Counselling Skills for Health Professionals.

Teaching Interpersonal Skills: A Handbook of Experiential Learning for Health Professionals.

Coping With Stress in the Health Professions.

Professional and Ethical Issues in Nursing: The Code of Professional Conduct (with C.M. Chapman).

Nurse Education: The Way Forward (with C.M. Chapman).

Nursing Research in Action: Developing Basic Skills (with P. Morrison).

Caring and Communicating: The Interpersonal Relationship in Nursing (with P. Morrison).

Caring and Communicating: The Interpersonal Relationship in Nursing: Facilitators' Manual (with P. Morrison).

Know Yourself! A Handbook of Self-Awareness Activities for Nurses.

Learning From Experience: Experiential Learning in Action.

Communication Skills for the Health Professional.

About the Author

Philip Burnard trained as a nurse and has worked in a variety of clinical settings. He has been a teacher and interpersonal skills trainer for 12 years and has a PhD in experiential learning. He is also an honourary lecturer in Nursing at the Hogeschool Midden Nederland, Utrecht, Netherlands. Author of more than 120 articles and papers, he has also published ten other books on counselling, education, research, ethics, stress and related issues. Dr Burnard is married with two children and lives in Caerphilly, South Wales. His interests include playing jazz piano, computing and writing.

Contents

Introduction

This book is written especially for all support workers and care assistants in the health care field. Health care is changing. Increasingly, support workers are relied upon to offer care in a wide range of health care settings. In those settings, communication with clients, with colleagues and with other workers is essential. Yet it is the communication aspect of the job that is most often glossed over. It is often assumed that people who work with other people are 'naturally' good at communicating. This book is for those who don't make that assumption. It is written for support workers, those who are undertaking college courses and those who need material for discussion and workshop facilitation.

We all communicate. In fact it is difficult to think of times when we are *not* communicating with other people. Therefore, the degree to which we can help others is largely dependent on our ability to communicate with them. The skills discussed and described in this book have wide application. Think, for a moment, about how YOU communicate in the following situations:

● You are going to work in a new setting for the first time. It is your first day.
● You are introduced to another member of the caring team.
● You are asked to write a brief report about something that has happened in the place where you work.
● You are asked to write a letter on a computer.
● Someone is rude to you and upsets you.
● Someone pays you a compliment.
● A client or a colleague starts to cry.
● Someone wants to talk to you about their problems at home.

How do you cope? Are all of the situations listed above easy ones to handle? Or do you sometimes come unstuck? Hopefully, the second possibility is the one you say 'yes' to: none of us is perfect when it comes to communication. On the other hand, we can all improve our communication skills. It is from this point of view that this book has been written. Its aim is to get you to reflect on your own skills, identify your strengths and deficits and then build new skills.

Who is this book for?

If you have read this far, it is probably for you. It is for anyone who is working in the health care field in a supportive role. It will be of help to, at least, the following groups of people:

- nursing support workers
- care assistants
- students on health care courses
- nursing auxiliaries and assistants
- voluntary workers in the health field
- telephone counsellors
- those who are working in health care and who want to improve their communication skills
- teachers, trainers and facilitators in the health care field.

The term 'health care field' is used to denote any of those occupations in which people are cared for or offered support, advice, medical or social help. Thus the term embraces nursing, social work, the paramedical professions, voluntary work and any other caring occupations. The skills described and discussed here are applicable to all of these settings.

The person who works in a support role in the health care field does a particularly important job. It is he or she who often spends most time with the client. Research has indicated that clients will often talk to non-professionally trained staff instead of highly trained professionals. There is evidence, too, that voluntary workers often make excellent lay counsellors because they do not bring a particular psychological view to the relationship but one that is more in keeping with the idea of 'befriending'.

To prevent confusion about different sorts of roles and different sorts of jobs, I have used the term 'health care support workers' throughout the book to denote any of the readers to whom I have referred above. I have also used the term 'health care worker' to refer to anyone who works in the field – professionally trained or otherwise.

The book will also be useful as a reference guide and manual of practical activities for trainers and teachers in the various parts of the health care field. The health care professions are, as ever, in a constant state of change. New courses are constantly being planned and old ones adapted. It is hoped that the book will offer some suggestions about how to run communication skills courses and spark off ideas about activities and exercises in such courses.

It will be helpful to those who have a managerial role in the caring and health arena as a stimulus for debate and discussion. In the end, we all need to become better communicators however broad or narrow our experience.

What is in this book?

The book covers a wide range of communication skills. It starts by considering what communication skills are and how we all use them. Some of the material in the early chapters is returned to, in greater depth, in later chapters. This is intentional. In the first place, it is important to 'flag up' certain basic skills. Later, it is important to explore those skills in detail.

The book goes on to look at verbal and non-verbal behaviour. It describes and discusses the skills involved in listening and talking to clients. Working with people on a one-to-one basis and in groups are both issues that are addressed. Then the focus shifts towards practical communication skills of a different sort: answering the telephone, writing and using computers. It closes with chapters on assertiveness and self-awareness.

No one ever learned skills simply by reading a book. This book has been designed to encourage you to interact with it. Each chapter contains a discussion of the topic and this is followed by the following aids to learning:

- a communication skills check list
- three activities for skills development
- a communication skills questionnaire
- a further reading list.

Throughout the book there are short extracts called 'Using the Skills: Spotting the Problem'. These offer examples of problems in communication related to the issues being discussed in the chapter. They encourage you to apply what you have read. The appendix also contains 40 activities for developing communication skills. Some you can do on your own, others involve you and another person, and some are for use in a small group. The book closes with an extensive bibliography of further books and articles related to communication.

I have purposely omitted references to the literature and research in the text, so that the book is easier to read. If you want to follow up the ideas in each chapter, the further reading lists and the bibliography will help. It can be taken as read, though, that the content of the book is drawn from the literature and research. In essence, my intention has been to make the book readable and above all, practical.

Most important of all, it is vital that you relate what is in the book to *your own experience*. You have been communicating a long time. You have already learned a great number of skills. I hope that this book encourages you to think about those skills, review them and then develop them further.

How do I use the book?

There are various ways of working through this book. Some may use it as part of a course and will be directed through it by course teachers. Others will want to select certain chapters to read first and perhaps to return to others at a later date. You can, of course, sit down and read straight through it. However, it is recommended that you go through it fairly slowly and that you *REFLECT* as you go.

If the book is used by trainers, it will be helpful if an **experiential learning model** of training is used with this book. That is to say, that the following stages are worked through:

● A theory input is given by the trainer.
● An activity from this or another book is played out by the learning group.
● The group reflect on the activity – in pairs or in small groups.
● Learning from the pairs or small groups is shared in a plenary session.
● The theory input and the learning from the exercise is linked through discussion.
● The members of the learning group try out their new skills in a real life setting, back at the workplace.

Communication skills cannot only be learned through reading a book on the topic. The skills described must be translated into action. They must be used *consciously*, too, even if, in the early stages, this makes the learner feel a bit awkward. I have noticed three stages in the learning of interpersonal skills:

● **Stage one**—the student has no idea of the range of communication skills available to him or her. All of the caring skills are assumed to 'come naturally'.
● **Stage two**—the student learns a range of communication skills, tries some of them out and suddenly becomes 'awkward' because they notice everything they do.
● **Stage three**—the student absorbs and adapts the various skills into their repertoire and these skills become 'natural' again. They are not thought about but they are practised in the workplace, with clients and colleagues.

Perhaps the mark of a truly skilled communicator, as with other sorts of skills, is that the skills are used effortlessly and easily. Such expertise, though, only comes after a lot of practice. Communication skills, like all others, have to be practised on a regular basis or we lose them.

The really important point about communication skills is this: if we are to improve the way that we communicate we have to *change*. We cannot change unless we notice what parts of us and our behaviour *need* to change. Thus, the suggestion that you read slowly. As you read, ask yourself how the issues in each chapter relate to you. Then listen to the answer. You have within you all the necessary attributes to make you a more effective communicator.

This book can only be an aid in the process; the rest is up to you. One thing is certain: the better we communicate with the people with whom and for whom we work, the better we are likely to enjoy the process and the better care we are likely to offer. In the end, all work in the caring field must be aimed at offering better care to clients.

A word about the use of language in this book. I have tried to make the book both readable and practical so I have tended to address the reader directly as 'you'. I have also struggled with sexist language and found no reasonable compromise. I am well aware of people's appropriate sensitivities to the use of 'he' and 'she' and have tried to deal with the issue as fairly as I can.

Finally, I have called the person whom the support worker cares for or looks after, the **client**. Again, this will not necessarily suit everyone. Some health care workers use the term 'patient', others 'resident' and still others 'consumer' or 'customer'. Some make the point that we should abandon such labels altogether and talk of the 'person'. It becomes clumsy, though, to write and read the 'patient/customer/resident/person' so I have plumped for 'client'.

Getting to know more about yourself is an exciting and sometimes risky business. I hope you will enjoy working through this book. If you have any suggestions to make about how it could be modified or improved, I would be glad to hear from you.

Philip Burnard
Caerphilly
Mid-Glamorgan

1
Communication in the Health Care Field

Keywords

- individuals
- families
- groups
- speaking
- non-verbal communication
- writing and computing
- ineffective communication

The main point of working in the health care field is to communicate. Whilst many other professions concentrate on consumer supply, health care workers are concerned with interpersonal relationships. Such relationships are many and varied.

First of all, the client who comes to the health care support worker lives in a certain context. He or she is or has been part of a family. That family is or has lived in a particular community. Not all of the members of the family may get on with each other. Within the family and within the local community there will be the usual arguments, feuds, disagreements and dislikes that go with any group of people living in proximity. Sometimes, this very fact is the thing that brings a person into contact with a health profession.

People live in particular contexts. This is as true for the health care support worker as it is for the client. The danger, of course, is that the health care support worker will fall into the trap of comparing the client's world with his or her own world. This may not be appropriate. Just as we are all different as individuals, so the ways that we choose to live as families and communities vary widely. We cannot assume that other people share our values, beliefs, feelings and thoughts. Nor can we assume that they share our prejudices, biases and so forth. Just as we as health care workers vary, so do the clients that we care for.

Throughout this book, the emphasis is on trying to understand the world of the other person. One essential method of doing this is to *listen* to the other person. Not just listen, but listen without prejudgement, without 'interpreting' what the other person 'really means'. None of us can mind-read and none of us can understand what is going on inside another person's head.

Some psychologists would have you believe otherwise: some psychotherapies, for example, are based on the idea that we can anticipate how other people's minds work. That approach is not taken in this book. Instead, the assumption is that we can learn to understand other people only by trying to enter their world with them. In doing this, we have to leave behind a lot of our own beliefs, judgements, prejudices and biases. This is no easy task. It does, however, make the job much more interesting. This book helps you to explore your own beliefs and values as a method of helping you to communicate with others.

Aspects of Communication

Communication is an essential part of our work. On reflection, it can be noted that we are communicating all of the time that we are with other people. We don't just communicate verbally. We communicate non-verbally, through gestures, facial expression, tones of voice and so forth. We also communicate via the choice of words and phrases that we use. Consider, for example, the following expressions. What do these 'say' about the other person?

● 'I, like, feel really good about all this. I mean, it really is great. You know what I mean?'
● 'I have a deep sense of wondering about where we are both at. I want to share with you my sense of wonderment at some of the things that I have experienced.'

- 'It is important for us both to be clear. I will try to tell you how I feel. Perhaps you can do the same.'
- 'It's good, isn't it? I like it a lot.'

These expressions all 'mean' roughly the same thing. The way they are put, however, indicate things about the people who say them. We communicate through our language and language style. This is worth thinking about in some detail. On the one hand, it is important to try to understand what another person means when they use a very different language style. On the other, it is important that we don't patronise people and try to adopt their language style when we speak to them. Recently, I tried to use some of the expressions that my 14-year-old son uses with his friends. This was the result:

'Don't even try, Dad.'
'Why?'
'Because even when you get the words right, it still doesn't sound right.'
'Why's that?'
'Because you're too old and because you're my Dad.'

You have to be credible in the language style that you use. If you are not, the chances are you will be rejected, to a greater or lesser degree, by the person you are talking to.

Other ways in which we communicate are through the accent that we have. Whilst, for a while in the UK, it was fashionable to try to drop regional accents, they are now being encouraged again and add a richness to conversations and to the language through their particular use of words and phrases. Again, it is important not to try to mimic the accent of the person you are with. Some people say that 'I just end up talking like them' when they are with someone who has a pronounced accent. This may be true but if you are secure in your own accent, it seems less likely to happen. Be you; don't try to imitate others.

Finally, in this short discussion of how we communicate, we need to consider physical appearance. As always, it can be deceiving. Not only do people vary in their weight, height and attractiveness, they also vary considerably in the way they dress. Some people consciously adopt particular styles of dress to conform to a particular group code. For a time, for instance, green waterproof coats were associated with yuppies; leather jackets of a certain sort have long been associated with motorbike riders.

It is easy to make mistakes, though. Not everyone who wears particular sorts of clothes is trying to join a club. Some people wear clothes of a certain sort just because they like them. Others just buy clothes because they think they are functional. Just as it is important to avoid too readily 'reading between the lines' in a conversation, so it is vital not to jump to conclusions about what a person's clothes 'say'. It is easy to get it wrong.

The Health Care Field

What are health care workers? A short list of people that might fall into this category follows; see if you can add to this list. Consider, also, if there is a hierarchy in this list. Are some health professionals viewed by society or by individuals as more important than others? Do some health professionals see themselves as more important than some of their colleagues?

Traditionally, the health professions *have* been hierarchical. There are all sorts of reasons for this that will not be discussed here. Suffice to say that the situation is changing. As people are becoming more aware of health issues and are demanding more of the health services, many health care workers are having to reassess their place in the hierarchy. This is also of direct importance to the issues in this book. As the general public becomes more questioning and critical of health services, so the need for effective communication skills is likely to grow. The list of some health care workers is as follows:

- doctors
- social workers
- nurses
- occupational therapists
- physiotherapists
- speech therapists
- remedial gymnasts
- psychotherapists
- voluntary workers
- counsellors
- dentists
- alternative therapists
- complimentary therapists.

Communication Within the Health Care Field

It is easy to become narrow-minded in your job, but what you do not only affects the client you are working with, it also has implications for other health care workers in other branches of the professions. Consider how much you are aware of who else has contact with the clients that you work with. How often do you meet those people?

Within the job that you do, the question of communication stretches fairly widely. First of all, there is the communication that takes place between the health professional and the client; this aspect of communication will be discussed at length in this book. Alongside this, we are communicating with our colleagues through discussions, conversations, meetings and groups. These, too, will be discussed later in the book. Once we go home, we talk to our families and friends; this, too, is an aspect of communication.

Finally, in the list of personal types of communication, we communicate with ourselves. At first sight, this seems an odd thing to read. On the other hand, reflect on the degree to which you have an almost continuous conversation going on inside your head. We are all continually reflecting on what we do and on how we do it. It is as though there is an internal censor at work, saying, as we live out our lives 'Is *this* right? . . . Is *this*. . .?' Part of developing this internal dialogue is the process of becoming self-aware; self-awareness has a chapter to itself.

Aspects of communication that are not of a face-to-face sort include using the telephone — a particular skill if it is done well. Also under this section, we need to think about written communication. What we write in reports, essays and notes all indicate not only things about that which we are writing but also things about ourselves. What we write says something about who we are. Just as we can all enhance our verbal communication skills, we can also brush up on our writing skills. Increasingly, writing is coming to mean computing. In another chapter of this book, we will consider how computers can aid the process of communication in the health services both for the individual and for the organisation.

Ineffective Communication

These, then, are the aspects of communication in the health care field. All of us, all of the time, need to think carefully about how to communicate with others. Consider, for example, the following snippets of conversation that can be heard in various parts of the health care field. All are an attempt to communicate with others. What is less clear is the degree to which they succeed as caring forms of communication. Read them through and consider what, if anything, could be improved upon. Consider then (and this is far more disturbing!) the degree to which you or your colleagues communicate in this way:

- 'Don't worry, dear, everything will work out all right. . .'
- 'If you're a P343, sit over there. . .'
- 'She was an appendix admitted last week. . .'
- 'Just have a teeny weeny bit more, lovely. . .'
- 'I'm not prepared to discuss that with you. . .'
- 'Do you really mean that?'
- 'We are only trying to help you, you know. . .'

- 'Don't get so emotional, it won't change anything. . .'
- 'I know what you mean, I'm just like that myself. . .'
- 'I can't talk to you now . . . you'll have to wait. . .'
- 'You've been through a lot, dear, haven't you?'
- 'I think you have to be prepared to take advice or we can't really help you. . .'
- 'It doesn't help to take that attitude. . .'

All of these examples represent, to a greater or lesser degree, breakdowns in communication. Not all of them are breakdowns of the same sort. Some show little thought about the person who is hearing them. Others indicate disrespect for the other person. Some suggest arrogance and insensitivity. In the end, there are many considerations to make when we talk to another person. Fortunately, most of them are easily learned.

Clear, effective and thoughtful communication is essential for all those who are responsible for working with and caring for other people. We can no longer 'make it up as we go along'. We need to be clear:

- why we are communicating
- what it is we are trying to communicate
- who we are communicating to
- how we are coping with that communication.

These issues are what this book is all about.

Communication Skills Check List

- All health care support workers work with individuals.
- Individuals live in a context that involves other people (families, communities, colleagues.
- We are communicating all of the time, whether we like it or not.
- We learned to communicate: we can learn to communicate better.
- There are certain types of communication that are best avoided.
- Communication can involve face-to-face encounters, group meetings, using the telephone and writing.
- When we communicate we say more about ourselves than just the words we use.

Activities for Skills Development

ACTIVITY ONE

Read through the following descriptions. Note what you tend to 'read into' those descriptions and the conclusions that you tend to draw.

Peter is 18. He has very long bleached hair. He wears one very large ear-ring, he also wears a number of rings on three of his fingers. He is dressed in torn jeans and a white tee-shirt that reads 'Guns and Roses'. His hands indicate that he is a heavy smoker. He swears a lot as he talks and tends to make little eye contact.

Mrs Jones is middle-aged. She wears dark clothes and heavy shoes. She talks very quietly and seems to have little to say. She carries with her a large shopping bag, which seems to be packed with various boxes.

David Andrews is 32. He was once a boxer. He is wearing a double-breasted suit and a bright tie. He has a deep tan. He also wears white socks that seem to clash with the black shoes that match his suit. He talks with an 'Oxford' accent.

Once you have read through these descriptions, consider the following proposition: *you cannot draw any conclusions about these people until you have met and talked to them*. If you can, discuss this proposition with other people perhaps as a group activity.

ACTIVITY TWO

Write out a description of yourself in the 'third person'. That is to say, start the description as follows:

Example
'David Green is 22. He works at . . .'

Try to make your description as complete as possible. Then read through your description and reflect on the insight that you have gained from viewing yourself in this way. If possible, show your description to other people and invite them to comment. Consider the degree to which your description of yourself highlights the sorts of things you notice in other people.

ACTIVITY THREE

Go to your college library and try to find as much information as possible about health care fields other than your own. If this proves difficult, ask the librarian where you could find such information. Try to familiarise yourself with the similarities and contrasts between those other health care fields and the one that you work in. To what degree do they do similar work to yours?

Communications Skills Questionnaire: Communication in the health care fields

Read through the items in the following questionnaire and tick the response that corresponds to how you feel about the statement. If you are working in a group, you may want to compare your responses to the statements. There are no right or wrong answers but the statements can help you to clarify your own thinking and beliefs about the topic.

1. It is possible to 'read people like a book' if you know how.

Strongly agree	Agree	Don't know	Disagree	Strongly disagree

2. Generally, I am fairly clear about how I appear to other people.

Strongly agree	Agree	Don't know	Disagree	Strongly disagree

3. Most health care workers communicate fairly clearly with their clients.

Strongly agree	Agree	Don't know	Disagree	Strongly disagree

4.It doesn't matter *how* you say things to people, it is *what* you say that matters.

Strongly agree	Agree	Don't know	Disagree	Strongly disagree

5. Most communication is common sense.

Strongly agree	Agree	Don't know	Disagree	Strongly disagree

6. It is important that clients feel equal in the health care worker–client relationship.

Strongly agree	Agree	Don't know	Disagree	Strongly disagree

7. Clients should be careful about their communication, too.

Strongly agree	Agree	Don't know	Disagree	Strongly disagree

8. Most of my colleagues are better communicators than me.

Strongly agree	Agree	Don't know	Disagree	Strongly disagree

9. I'm not sure that you can *learn* to be a more effective communicator.

Strongly agree	Agree	Don't know	Disagree	Strongly disagree

10. Personal experience has a lot to do with how we communicate with others.

Strongly agree	Agree	Don't know	Disagree	Strongly disagree

Further Reading

Allan, J. 1989 *How to Develop Your Personal Management Skills*. Kogan Page, London.

Burnard, P. 1989 *Teaching Interpersonal Skills: A Handbook of Experiential Learning for Health Professionals*. Chapman and Hall, London.

Robertson, I.T. and Cooper, C.L. 1983 *Human Behaviour in Organisations*. Pitman Press, London.

2
Communication Skills: What are they?

Keywords

- listening
- talking
- non-verbal communication
- other communication skills
- cultural differences.

This chapter explores the basic elements of face-to-face communication with other people. It starts by considering ways of enhancing the ability to listen. It continues with a discussion of the skills involved in talking to other people in a therapeutic way and then continues with a short discussion of non-verbal communication before considering groups, personal values and the importance of respecting other peoples' values. Many of the issues discussed in this chapter will be returned to for a more detailed discussion in later chapters.

Listening

Listening to others is the crux of working in the health care field. If we can listen and not judge or condemn (or even disagree with) others, we are already working in a therapeutic way.

Consider the following example of a conversation and think about what happens in it. The first person is talking to the other but the other is not really listening to the first. What happens as a result? Think, too, about whether or not you often find yourself in conversations of this sort. If you are on the receiving end of such a conversation, does it help you? If you are on the listening end, how could you be more helpful? As you read through this conversation, imagine how it could be improved upon:

'I feel really awful, my girlfriend has given me up and I've just lost my job'.

'I'm sure she'll be back. . .'

'She never really liked me much anyway.'

'That can't be true! She wouldn't have gone out with you at all if that was the case.'

'No. She didn't really like me. I liked her a lot though. It's upset me more than I thought it would.'

'You shouldn't think about her like that. It's not fair to her. I'm sure she wouldn't have gone out with you if she didn't like you.'

'How would you know, anyway?'

'Sorry. I was only trying to help. If you are going to get shirty, perhaps I better get going.'

Have you heard conversations like that? Most of us have been involved in them fairly often. The point is that such conversations are not particularly productive because the person who is doing the talking is *not being listened to*. Listening, then, is the most important element of face-to-face conversation.

Consider the next example of how the above conversation *might* have been. Try to spot how it differs from the first example and why it seems to 'work' better. Try, particularly, to identify the specific elements that make it more effective.

'I feel really awful, my girlfriend has given me up and I've just lost my job.'

'You sound as though you've had a lot going wrong for you. . .'

'I could have put up with my girlfriend going . . . it's just that I don't think she ever really liked me anyway. . .'

'Did she ever tell you that?'

'No. Just the opposite . . . she reckoned she liked me a lot. Ha! I see what you mean . . . I suppose she *did* like me. . .'

'Yet she gave you up?'

'Well, sort of. We had an argument and we disagreed on all sorts of things. . .'

'So she didn't actually give you up?'

'No. I suppose not, really. I suppose I could phone her and sort something out. I suppose I just thought she wouldn't want to see me again. What with losing my job as well. Before, we used to get on really well. I suppose I haven't been at all easy to talk to for the last couple of weeks. I've had a lot on my mind. I think I *will* give her a ring. Listen: I'll see you again soon. Thanks a lot!'

Think about the differences between the two extracts and consider, in each case, the following issues:

● who did the most *talking*?
● how did the 'listener' *respond*?
● what sorts of things did the listener *say*?
● how did the 'talker' respond to what the listener had to say?
● what was the difference in outcome?

If we think about listening as a *process*, as a series of activities that enable the other person to understand themselves a bit more and to be able to think things through for themselves, we can immediately identify things that the listener should *not* do. The listener should avoid:

● arguing with the other person
● avoiding what the other person is saying
● imposing his or her own values on the other person
● overtalking.

Arguing while the other person is trying to talk is rarely productive, especially in the early stages of a relationship. It rarely helps to tell a client that they are mistaken in what they say — particularly when they are talking about themselves. It is very easy to find yourself saying these sorts of things (but they are rarely helpful):

● 'Don't be silly, of course you're not'
● 'I don't see it that way'
● 'I'm sure that's wrong . . .' and so on.

In the early stages of listening, then, *acceptance* of the other person is of foremost importance. It is this sort of acceptance that allows us to begin to understand the other person's world-view. If we accept what they say as representing how they see the world, we begin to enter their 'frame of reference', their way of seeing things. Later, as we get to know them better, we can begin to gently disagree or challenge.

Initially, though, the emphasis is on listening and accepting. This is best done by simply sitting and allowing the other person to talk. A good listener does not talk very much. This may seem an obvious point, but listen to some of the people who tell you that they are 'good listeners': in my experience, many of them really mean that they are 'good talkers'. Good listening, like all other skills, takes practice. It will be useful if we begin by considering some of the specific behavioural skills that go with effective listening.

Behavioural Aspects of Listening

Think, first, about how you sit or stand in relation to the person that you are listening to. It usually helps to sit or stand almost exactly opposite them. In that way, you not only hear what they say but you also *see* them. We take in a lot of information about other people through looking at them. Whilst it is important not to try to 'interpret' peoples' body language (and we will discuss that again later, see page 30) it is important that we can see their changing expressions and gestures. First, then, sit or stand opposite the other person.

Second, think about eye contact. Some would have us believe that the eyes are the windows of the soul, and they certainly help to make us more expressive. Notice, too, that there are times when we do not or cannot make eye contact. If we are embarrassed, angry, shy or defensive, we may find such contact difficult. Again, if we are sitting opposite the person who is talking, we are in a better position to see the changing quality of the other person's eye contact. Also, we are in a better position to *make* eye contact with the other person. For it is through such eye contact that we make ourselves available to the other person. We demonstrate acceptance and friendliness through making eye contact.

Perhaps the use of eye contact is one of the most essential skills in the process of listening. It certainly makes a difference to the person who is talking. Try this simple experiment. Next time a friend is talking to you, avoid his or her eye. Just notice how quickly the conversation dries up. Then, with another friend, try increasing the amount of eye contact you make and note the consequences.

The third skill in listening to the other person is that of maintaining an 'open' position. You are in an open position when you are not folding your arms or legs. A closed position is exactly the opposite — you have your arms folded and your legs crossed. Now, in Western culture, it is common for people to cross their legs when they sit down. The totally closed position, though, can indicate lack of interest or defensiveness.

It is suggested that if it is possible to sit comfortably in a completely open position, you are more likely to convey a welcoming and 'listening' attitude towards the other person. Again, as with the previous skill, try this out with a friend. See how he or she responds to both a closed and an open position.

A fourth and final skill in this short list is learning to relax. Very often, when we listen to another person, we only give them half our attention. The other half is taken up with working out what *we* are going to say next. Instead of doing this, try to relax and even to remain 'empty headed' about what your response will be. Trust yourself that you will be able to say something reasonable when the times comes. What you may find is that you have less to say and this, in turn, encourages the other person to say more. This, after all, is the aim of the exercise.

We probably all talk more than we have to. Most of us like the sound of our own voices and think that what we have to say is important. In a therapeutic conversation, what is important is what the client has to say. What we have to say comes a long way second. Try, if you can, to say less to clients and let them say more.

Talking

We take talking for granted. We all do it so, presumably, we all think we do it quite well. All I want to suggest, in this section, is that you *listen* to yourself and other people talking. You will be quite shocked by what you hear – especially if you listen to yourself. If you can bear it, listen to a recording of yourself on tape. If possible, too, watch and listen to yourself on video. If you are on a course, this may be a required part of that course. Whilst watching and listening to yourself in this way is often quite disturbing at the time, it is possible to learn a lot from it.

Pay particular attention to the following list of issues, which all have a bearing on how we communicate with others. These issues affect the way that we convey what we mean to others and also the way in which other people 'take' to us. Like it or not, people tend to judge us a little by the way that we talk. That is not to suggest that we should all talk with the same sort of accent and in the same sort of way. It is merely to note that we can all do much to improve the way that we talk. We can all make ourselves more interesting through the way that we talk:

- tone of voice
- volume
- facial expression whilst talking
- use of arm and hand gestures
- actual words used (this is sometimes referred to as the 'language register'. Think for a moment, do you use simple words to convey what you mean or do you get caught up with unnecessarily long words or with jargon? Generally, simpler words are to be preferred to longer)
- eye contact whilst talking (or lack of it).

Now think of someone who you consider speaks well. What is it that makes you come to that conclusion? It is probably not (as we have discussed above) their accent. It is more likely to be that they speak reasonably slowly, clearly and that they *modulate* or vary their voice. Also, of course, they are likely to talk about interesting things.

Think about the sorts of things that you talk to other people about. Do you account for the listener's interests or do you tend to talk only about those things that interest you? One of my interests is computing; I can talk for hours to certain friends about computers. Usually, though, I can only talk to other friends for a few moments before they start yawning. Computers, like so many other things, are very boring if you don't happen to be interested in them.

When you talk, try to be interesting. Better still, try to talk about things that other people want to talk about. This links well with the paragraphs, above, on listening. As a health care worker, it is probably far more important to be a good listener than it is to be a good talker. The good listener will always be in demand.

Non-verbal Communication

We communicate to some degree with words. We communicate to a large degree with our bodies. That is to say that we communicate non-verbally. It is usually thought that we communicate *more* through the non-verbal aspects of our behaviour than we do through speech. Let's consider some of the aspects of non-verbal communication that we can use. A list of such aspects would include:

- eye contact
- facial expression
- hand gestures
- head nods
- proximity to others (how close we stand to them)
- touch
- all the aspects of speech that are not words themselves ('um's' and 'ah's', tone, volume, emphases and so on).

We have discussed a number of these in the sections on listening and talking. But for now, try to observe other people more closely by paying attention to these non-verbal aspects of communication. A word of warning, though. Despite what some books might say, it is not possible to *read* non-verbal communication. Whilst we might like to take guesses at what people 'really' mean by observing what their bodies appear to be 'saying', such interpretation is rarely accurate.

Consider, for example, someone who stands in front of you with their arms folded as they talk. Some of the books will tell you that this is a classic defensive position. But there are all sorts of other possibilities. A short list of 'other' interpretations might include:

- they are cold
- they are worried that you might notice they bite their nails
- they always stand like that
- they have a stomach ache.

The point is that there are nearly always numerous possibilities for why people move their bodies in particular ways. We would do well to steer clear of being too clever about how we interpret non-verbal behaviour. We can, however, **notice** it and respond to it. As we get to know people, so we get to understand their own personal 'body language' — it varies a lot from person to person. If in doubt, though, there is one simple rule. If you want to know something about someone: ask them. Just that. Don't assume things about people, ask them instead. It is nearly always far safer than making assumptions.

All these issues are developed in more detail in the next chapter. For now, all that is necessary is to underline the importance of listening as a therapeutic activity in the health care field. If you can learn to listen well, you are already on the way to being an expert as a support worker.

Individuals

Other chapters discuss the details of working and communicating with others. In this opening discussion about the nature of communication, it is important to begin to think about those factors that make or break one-to-one relationships. Think about people that you regularly meet on a one-to-one basis. Think about *why* you meet them. A shortlist of factors that come into play when two people meet includes:

- **First impressions** — sometimes these are lasting. If they are *not*, and impressions change, it is rare for the person to return to their original impressions of the person. In other words, if you start out disliking someone and you subsequently grow to like them, it is unlikely that you will *return* to disliking them.
- **Reciprocity** — this is a clumsy word that refers to the degree to which interest is mutual. If I meet you, like you and treat you well, the chances are that you will return those things. Reciprocity in relationships makes for good relationships.

- **Attraction** — consider the people that you like. Do you also find them attractive? If this happens when you meet a client, you need to think about your responsibility for accepting this fact but not acting on it.
- **Projection** — we often see in others qualities that we have ourselves but of which we are unaware. In other words, if I am a talkative person but do not know that, I might see 'talkativeness' in others. We often project negative qualities onto other people but sometimes we also see *good* qualities that are also our own.
- **Time** — the longer we know someone, the more likely we are to get on with them. Many relationships cannot be rushed. We cannot force people to like us nor can we rush them to disclose themselves to us. One-to-one relationships take time to develop.

How do these factors in one-to-one relationships relate to relationships in your own life? Consider, too, whether you agree with the list and whether you could add to it. In later chapters, we will consider one-to-one relationships in greater detail

Groups

We all live and work in the company of others — we all live and work in groups. This is a fact, whether we like it or not. Consider, for a moment, the degree to which you *like* working in groups. Consider, then, how you feel when you most decidedly *are* working in groups. Think back to group work in school and college. Did you enjoy that sort of learning experience? Think, then, about discussion groups and meetings. Again, consider whether or not you feel yourself to be comfortable working directly in groups.

One thing is for sure: we act differently in groups than we do in one-to-one relationships. Factors to consider when thinking about groups and group work are:

- **Size** — it is quite different to work and talk in a group of five people than it is to work and talk in a group of thirty.
- **Status** — you may find it easier to talk in a group if you are a high status person. Alternatively, you may find it difficult to talk in a group if you feel that your status is not very high.
- **Purpose** — why has the group met? Do you know your own role in the group? If so, are you happy and confident in that role?
- **Timing** — groups get easier to work in as we gain experience of them. As we get to know the group membership we are more likely to settle down and find talking easier.

The Needs of Others

Working in the health care field means thinking about the needs of others. The important question, here, is **who defines the needs of others**? It is possible to imagine that the qualified professional health care worker is well able to identify those needs. Clearly, though, after a little thought, it becomes apparent that, in most circumstances, it is **the person, him- or herself, that is best able to identify his or her needs.**

This issue of listening to the other person and allowing him or her to tell you what he or she needs is a vital aspect of all health care work. In the end, only *you* are an expert on *you:* you are not an expert on other people, nor they on you.

Your Own Needs

Underneath all this work with others, lie our own needs. It is important, as you learn to communicate more effectively with others, to remember that you, too, have needs that are sometimes satisfied and sometimes not. It is vital that they do not get overlooked entirely in the rush to care for others. As an introduction to this topic, think about the following questions:

- Why do you work in a health care field?
- How do you benefit from your work?
- What are you learning about yourself?
- What would you lose if you did not do this work?

Questions like this can help in the process of values clarification, the process of developing self-awareness and a greater understanding of personal needs.

Enhancing Communication

How can we learn to be better at communicating with others? Clearly, some of the skills are learned through college or training courses. Others are learned by observing others at work. We learn from good role models but we also learn from bad ones. Sometimes, though, we learn through reflecting on what we see and what we do. Stop for a moment, and consider your own strengths and deficits as a communicator. Try to identify what else you need to do to enhance your communication skills. The rest of this book is dedicated to encouraging you to constantly review and refine your skills. The more you reflect on what you do, the more it will become clear what else you *need* to do.

Other Types of Communication

So far, the discussion in this book has focused on direct communication between two or more people. When we talk about communication, we often use the term in this sense. It is important, in closing this chapter, to consider some of the other ways that we communicate. Briefly these are:

- through writing
- through computing
- through use of the telephone.

Each of these different sorts of communication is considered in this book. To be an effective communicator we need to be fluent in each of these aspects. Communication is always broader than a conversation or a group discussion. When we write to another person or answer the phone, we represent the profession that we work for. It is important that we convey a positive and effective image.

Cultural Differences

Cultures, like societies, differ from one another. Many of the issues discussed in this chapter are *culture specific*. That is to say that the verbal and non-verbal behaviours identified here are used specifically in Western countries, and even more specifically in North America and the UK. You cannot assume that what is true about non-verbal behaviour and about styles of talking in Britain will be true in other cultures.

Therefore it is vitally important to learn to quickly recognize the non-verbal and verbal rules of other cultures. Britain is now multicultural. It is neither appropriate nor desirable to force other cultures to use the same communication styles as British people: nor is it likely to be possible. Observe, then, people from other cultures and avoid drawing conclusions from what you observe. For example, mutual eye contact is not a universal phenomenon. In many parts of the Middle and Far East, it is considered rude to make direct eye contact with someone who is in a senior position to you. Thus, it should not be thought that someone from the Far East who does not make direct eye contact is being rude or inattentive – far from it. In fact, they are being polite.

The idea that the British way of communicating is the *right* way is an example of *ethnocentricity* – the belief that any given culture does things correctly, whilst all other cultures are somehow 'wrong'. Try to notice any tendency within yourself or your colleagues towards ethnocentricity.

Communication Skills Check List

●   We all need to learn to listen more effectively.

●   Communication skills training involves working with individuals and groups.

●   We learn a lot about ourselves as we learn to communicate more effectively.

Activities for Skills Development

ACTIVITY ONE

Observe people this week. Notice to what degree you read 'meaning' into what they say and do. Then reflect on whether or not the interpretation that you make is likely to be accurate.

ACTIVITY TWO

Listen to the way that other colleagues talk about clients. Do they interpret what other people do? If so, what is the basis of that interpretation?

ACTIVITY THREE

Go to the library and search for books on interpersonal behaviour and on non-verbal communication. Become familiar with the sorts of books that are available, from the popular to the academic. Which do you think are going to be most useful to you as a health care worker?

Communication Skills Questionnaire: Aspects of communication skills

Read through the items in the following questionnaire and tick the response that corresponds to how you feel about the statement. If you are working in a group, you may want to compare your responses to the statements. There are no right or wrong answers but the statements can help you to clarify your own thinking and beliefs about the topic.

1. Most people in the health care field are fairly good listeners.

Strongly agree	Agree	Don't know	Disagree	Strongly disagree

2. I am better at listening than most of my friends.

Strongly agree	Agree	Don't know	Disagree	Strongly disagree

3. You can't *learn* to be a good listener.

Strongly agree	Agree	Don't know	Disagree	Strongly disagree

4. Listening skills are the most important ones in communication studies.

Strongly agree	Agree	Don't know	Disagree	Strongly disagree

5. It is important to learn to 'read a person like a book'.

Strongly agree	Agree	Don't know	Disagree	Strongly disagree

6. It is easy to learn to read peoples' body language.

Strongly agree	Agree	Don't know	Disagree	Strongly disagree

7. In a meeting between two people, it is important that the talking is shared about 50 – 50 between them.

Strongly agree	Agree	Don't know	Disagree	Strongly disagree

8. I don't think I could ever work effectively in a group where I had to do a lot of talking.

Strongly agree	Agree	Don't know	Disagree	Strongly disagree

9. I could easily run a group.

Strongly agree	Agree	Don't know	Disagree	Strongly disagree

10. I know myself quite well when it comes to talking and listening.

Strongly agree	Agree	Don't know	Disagree	Strongly disagree

Further Reading

Argyle, M. 1978 *The Psychology of Interpersonal Behaviour.* Penguin, Harmondsworth, Middlesex.
Bond, M. 1985 *Stress and Self-Awareness.* Heinemann, London.
Burnard, P. 1990 *Learning Human Skills*, 2nd edn. Heinemann, Oxford.

3
Listening to people

KEYWORDS

- attending
- listening
- listening behaviour
- blocks to listening.

To listen to another person is the most caring act of all. Listening and attending are by far the most important aspects of being a health care worker. Everyone needs to be listened to. Unfortunately, most of us feel that we are obliged to talk! Unfortunately, too, it is 'overtalking' by the health care worker that is least productive.

If we can train ourselves to give our full attention to and really listen to the other person, we can do much to help them. First, we need to discriminate between the two processes: attending and listening.

Attending

Attending is the act of truly focusing on the other person. It involves consciously making ourselves aware of what the other person is saying and of what they are trying to communicate to us. Figure 3.1 demonstrates three hypothetical zones of attention. The zones may help to further clarify this concept of attending and has implications for improving the quality of attention offered to the client.

The 'Outside' Experience	The 'Inside' Experience
Zone one Attention 'out': focused on the outside world and on the client. When attention is focused out, the listener is *really* listening.	Zone two Attention 'in': focused on the listener's own thoughts and feelings. The listener is distracted and not able to listen fully.
	Zone three Attention focused on 'fantasy': what *might* be the case . . . The listener is busy playing the amateur psychotherapist.

Figure 3.1 Three possible zones of attention.

Zone one represents the zone of having our attention fully focused 'outside' ourself and on the environment around us or, in the context of health care work, on the client. When we have our attention fully focused 'out' in this way, we are fully aware of the other person and not distracted by our own thoughts and feelings.

There are some simple activities, borrowed from meditation practice, that can help and enhance our ability to offer this sort of attention. Here is a particularly straightforward one. Stop reading this book for a moment and allow your attention to focus on an object in the room that you are in: it may be a clock, or a picture or a piece of furniture — anything.

Focus your attention on the object and notice every aspect of it: its shape, its colour, its size and so forth. Continue to do this for at least one minute. Notice as you do this, how your attention becomes fully absorbed by the object. You have focused your attention 'out'. Then discontinue your close observation. Notice what is going on in your mind. What are your thoughts and feelings at the moment? When you do this, you have shifted your attention to zone two — the 'internal' domain of thoughts and feelings. Now shift the focus of your attention out again and onto another object. Study every aspect of it again for about a minute. Notice, as you do this, how it is possible to consciously and awarely shift the focus of your attention in this way.

You can will yourself to focus your attention outside yourself. Practice at this conscious process will improve your ability to fully focus outside yourself and onto the client.

If we are to pay close attention to every aspect of the client, it is important to be able to move freely between zones one and two. In practice, what probably happens when we are talking to another person is that we spend some time in zone one, paying full attention to the client and then we shuttle back into zone two and notice our reactions, feelings and beliefs about what they are saying, before we shift our attention back out.

The important thing is that we learn to gain control over this process. It is no longer a haphazard, hit and miss, affair but we can learn to focus attention with some precision. It is not until we train ourselves to consciously focus attention 'out' in this way that we can really notice what the other person is saying and doing.

Zone three in the diagram involves fantasy — ideas and beliefs that we have that bear no direct relation to what is going on at the moment but concerns what we think or believe is going on. When we listen to another person, it is quite possible to think and believe all sorts of things about them. We may, for example, think 'I know what he's really trying to tell me. He's trying to say that he doesn't want to go back to work, only he won't admit it — even to himself!'

When we engage in this sort of 'internal dialogue' we are working within the domain of fantasy. We cannot 'know' other things about people, unless we ask them. We often think that we know what another person thinks or feels, without checking with that person first. If we do this, it is because we are focusing on the zone of fantasy — we are engaged in the processes of attribution or interpretation.

The problem with these sorts of processes is that, if they are wrong, we stand to develop a very distorted picture of the other person! Our assumptions naturally lead us to other assumptions and if we begin to ask questions directly generated by those assumptions, our conversations will lack clarity and our client will end up very confused!

A useful rule, then, is that if we find ourselves within the domain of fantasy and we are 'inventing' things about the person in front of us, we stop and if necessary check those inventions with the client to test the validity of them. If the client confirms them, all well and good: we have intuitively picked up something about the client that he was, perhaps, not consciously or overtly telling us. If, on the other hand, we are wrong, it is probably best to abandon the fantasy all together. The fantasy, invention or assumption probably tells us more about our own mental make up than it does about that of our client! In fact, these 'wrong' assumptions can serve to help us gain more self-awareness. In noticing the wrong assumptions we make about others, we can reflect on what those assumptions tell us about ourselves.

Awareness of focus of attention and its shift between the three zones has implications for all aspects of listening and talking to people. The health care worker who is able to keep attention directed out for long periods is likely to be more observant and more accurate than the health care worker who is not. The health care worker who can discriminate between the zone of thinking and the zone of fantasy is less likely to jump to conclusions about their observations or to make value-judgements based on interpretation rather than on fact.

What is being suggested here is that we learn to focus directly on the other person (zone one) with occasional moves to the domain of our own thoughts and feelings (zone two) but that we learn, also, to attempt to avoid the domain of fantasy (zone three). It is almost as though we learn to meet the client as a 'blank slate': we know little about them until they tell us who they are. To work in this way in health care work is, almost paradoxically, a much more emphatic way of working. We learn, rapidly, not to assume things about the other person but to listen to them and to check out any hunches or intuitions we may have about them.

Being able to focus on zone one and have our attention focused out has other advantages. In focusing in this way, we can learn to maintain the 'therapeutic distance'. We can learn to distinguish clearly between what are the client's problems and what are our own. It is only when we become mixed up by having our attention partly focused on the client, partly on our own thoughts and feelings and partly on our fantasies and interpretations that we begin to get confused about what the client is telling us and what we are 'saying to ourselves'. We easily confuse our own problems with those of the client.

Second, we can use the concept of the three domains of attention to develop self-awareness. By noticing the times when we have great difficulty in focusing attention 'out', we can learn to notice points of stress and difficulty in our own lives.

Typically, we will find it difficult to focus attention out when we are tired, under pressure or emotionally distressed. The lack of attention that we experience can come to serve as a signal that we need to stop and take stock of our own life situation. Further, by allowing ourselves consciously to focus 'in' on zones two and three — the process of introspection — we can examine our thoughts and feelings in order to further understand our own make up. Indeed, this process of self-exploration seems to be essential if we are able to offer another person sustained attention.

If we constantly 'bottle-up' problems we will find ourselves distracted by what the client has to say. Typically, when they begin to talk of a problem of theirs that is also a problem for us, we will suddenly find our attention distracted to zone two: suddenly we will find ourselves pondering on our own problems and not those of the client! Regular self-examination can help us to clear away, at least temporarily, some of the more pressing personal problems that we experience.

Such exploration can be carried out either in isolation, in pairs or in groups.

If done in isolation, meditative techniques can be of value. Often, however, the preference will be to conduct such exploration in pairs or groups. In this way, we gain further insight through hearing other people's thoughts, feelings and observations and we can make useful comparisons between other people's experience and our own.

Listening

Listening is the process of 'hearing' the other person. This involves not only noting the things that they say but also a whole range of other aspects of communication.

Given the wide range of ways in which one person tries to communicate with another, this is further evidence of the need to develop the ability to offer close and sustained attention, as outlined above. There are three aspects of listening:

- linguistic aspects
- paralinguistic aspects
- non-verbal aspects.

Linguistic aspects of speech refer to the actual words that the client uses, to the phrases they choose and to the metaphors they use to convey how they are feeling.

Paralinguistics refers to all those aspects of speech that are not words, themselves. Thus, timing, volume, pitch, accent are all paralinguistic aspects of communication. Again, they can offer us indicators of how the other person is feeling beyond the words that they use. Again, however, we must be careful of making assumptions and slipping into zone three, the zone of fantasy. Paralinguistics can only offer us a possible clue to how the other person is feeling. It is important that we check with the client the degree to which that clue matches with the client's own perception of the way they feel.

Non-verbal aspects of communication refer to 'body language' — the way that the client expressed himself through the use of his body. Thus, facial expression, use of gestures, body position and movement, proximity to the health care worker and touch in relation to the counsellor, all offer further clues about the client's internal status beyond the words they use and can be 'listened' to by the attentive health care worker. Again, any assumptions that we make about what such body language 'means' need to be clarified with the client.

There is a temptation to believe that body language can be 'read', as if we all used it in the same sort of way. This is, perhaps, encouraged by works such as Desmond Morris's *Manwatching*. Reflection on the subject, however, will reveal that body language is dependent to a large degree on a wide number of variables: the context in which it occurs, the nature of the relationship, the individual's personal style and preference, the personality of the person 'using' the body language, and so on.

It is safer, therefore, not to assume that we 'know' what another person is 'saying' with their body language but to, again, treat it as a clue and to clarify with the client what he means by his use of it.

It is preferable, in listening to others, to merely bring to the client's attention the way they are sitting, or their facial expression, rather than to offer an interpretation of it. Two examples may help here. In the first, the health care worker is offering an interpretation and an assumption:

'I notice from the way that you have your arms folded and from your frown that you are uncomfortable with discussing things at home.'

In the second example, the health care worker merely feeds back observation to the client and allows the client to clarify his situation:

'I notice that you have your arms folded and that you're frowning. What are you feeling at the moment?'

Levels of Listening

The skilled health care worker learns to listen to all three aspects of communication and tries to resist the temptation to interpret what they hear. The three levels of listening and their components are:

- **Linguistic aspects** — words, phrases, metaphors, etc.
- **Paralinguistic aspects** — timing, volume, pitch, accent, 'ums and errs', fluency, etc.
- **Non-verbal aspects** — facial expression, use of gesture, touch, body position, proximity to the health care worker, body movement, eye contact, etc.

The first level of listening refers to the idea of the health care worker merely noting what is being said. In this mode, neither client nor health care worker are psychologically very 'close' and arguably the relationship will not develop very much. In the second level of listening the health care worker learns to develop 'free-floating' attention and listens 'overall' to what is being said, as opposed to trying to catch every word.

Free-floating attention also refers to 'going with' the client, of not trying to keep the client to a particular theme but of following their conversation wherever it goes. The health care worker also 'listens' to the client's non-verbal and paralinguistic behaviour as indicators of what the client is thinking and feeling.

Faced with this deeper level of listening, the client feels a greater amount of empathy being offered by the health care worker. The health care worker begins to enter the frame of reference of the client and to explore his perceptual world — they begin to see the world as the client experiences it.

In the third level of listening, the health care worker maintains free-floating attention, notices non-verbal and paralinguistic aspects of communication but also notices their own internal thoughts, feelings and body sensations. It is frequently the case that what the health worker is feeling, once the relationship has deepened, is a direct mirror image of what the client is feeling.

Thus, by noticing their own changes and gently checking these with the client, the health care worker is both listening to the client and using themselves as a sounding board for how the relationship is developing.

Use of 'Minimal Prompts'

While listening to the client, it is important that the health care worker *shows* that they are listening. An obvious aid to this is the use of what may be described as 'minimal prompts' — the use of head nods, 'yes's', 'mm's' and so on. All of these indicate that 'I am with you.' On the other hand, overuse can be irritating to the client, particularly, perhaps, the thoughtless and repetitive nodding of the head — the 'dog in the back of the car' phenomenon!

It is important that the health care worker, at least initially, is consciously aware of their use of minimal prompts and tries to vary their repertoire. It is important to note also, that very often such prompts are not necessary at all. Often, all the client needs is to be listened to, and they appreciate that the health care worker is listening, without the need for further reinforcement of the fact.

Behavioural Aspects of Listening

One other consideration needs to be made regarding the process of listening — the behaviour the health care worker adopts when listening to the client. Egan (1990) offers the acronym SOLER as a means of identifying and remembering the sorts of counsellor behaviour that encourage effective listening. The acronym is used as follows:

- sit **S**quarely in relation to the client
- maintain an **O**pen position
- **L**ean slightly towards the client
- maintain reasonable **E**ye contact with the client
- **R**elax!

First, the health care worker is encouraged to sit squarely in relation to the client. This can be understood both literally and metaphorically. In North America and the UK it is generally acknowledged that a person listens to another more effectively if they sit opposite or nearly opposite the other person, rather than next to them. Sitting opposite allows the health care worker to see all aspects of communication, both paralinguistic and non-verbal, that might be missed if they sat next to the client.

Second, the health care worker should consider adopting an open position in relation to the client. Again, this can be understood both literally and metaphorically. A 'closed' attitude is as much a block to effective conversation as is a closed body position. Crossed arms and legs, however, can convey a defensive feeling to the client and communication is often more effective if the health care worker sits without crossing either.

Having said that, many people feel more comfortable sitting with their legs crossed, so perhaps some license should be used here! What should be avoided is the position where the health care worker sits in a 'knotted' position with both arms and legs crossed.

It is helpful if the health care worker appreciates that they can lean towards the client. This can encourage the client and make them feel more understood. If this does not seem immediately clear, next time you talk to someone, try leaning away from the other person and note the result!

Eye contact with the client should be reasonably sustained and a good rule of thumb is that the amount of eye contact that the health care worker uses should roughly match the amount the client uses. It is important, however, that the health care worker's eyes should be 'available' for the client: the health care worker should always be prepared to maintain eye contact. On the other hand it is important that the client does not feel stared at and intimidated by the health care worker's glare.

Conscious use of eye contact can ensure that the client feels listened to and understood but not uncomfortable.

The amount of eye contact the health care worker can make will depend on a number of factors, including the topic under discussion, the degree of 'comfortableness' the health care worker feels with the client, the degree to which the health care worker feels attracted to the client, the amount of eye contact the client makes, the nature and quality of the client's eye contact and so forth.

If the health care worker continually finds the maintenance of eye contact difficult it is, perhaps, useful to consider talking the issue over with a trusted colleague or with a peer support group, for eye contact is a vital channel of communication in most interpersonal encounters.

Finally, it is important that the health care worker feels relaxed while listening. This usually means that they should refrain from 'rehearsing responses'. It means that the health care worker is completely given up to the task of listening and trusts that they will make an appropriate response when they have to. This underlines the need to consider listening as the most important aspect of communication. Everything else is secondary to it.

Many people feel that they have to have a ready response when engaged in a conversation with another person. In health care work, however, the main focus of the conversation is the client. The health care worker's verbal responses, although important, must be secondary to what the client has to say. Thus all the health care worker has to do is to sit back and intently listen. Easily said but not so easily done! The temptation to 'overtalk' is often great but can lessen with more experience and with the making of a conscious decision not to make too many verbal interventions.

All of these behavioural considerations can help the listening process. To be effective, however, they need to be used consciously. The health care worker needs to pay attention to using them and choose to use them. As we have noted, at first this conscious use of self will feel uncomfortable and unnatural.

Practice makes it easier and with that practice comes the development of the health care worker's own style of working and behaving in the caring relationship. No such style can develop if, first, the health care worker does not consciously consider the way they sit and the way they listen.

In summary, it is possible to identify some of those things that act as blocks to effective listening and some aids to effective listening. No doubt the reader can add to both of these lists and such additions will be useful in that they will be a reflection of your own strengths and limitations as a listener.

Blocks to Effective Listening

- the health care worker's own problems
- health care worker stress and anxiety
- awkward/uncomfortable seating
- lack of attention to listening behaviour
- value-judgements and interpretations on the part of the health care worker
- health care worker's attention focused 'in' rather than 'out'
- 'rehearsals' inside the health care worker's head.

Aids to Effective Listening

- attention focused 'out'
- suspension of judgement by the health care worker
- attention to the behavioural aspects of listening
- comfortable seating
- avoidance of interpretation
- judicious use of minimal prompts.

Communication Skills Check List

● Listening is the most important aspect of communicating with another person.

● Attending refers to giving your *whole* attention to the other person,

● Practice can improve our ability to offer attention.

● The behavioural aspects of listening can be remembered with the acronym SOLER.

Activities for Skills Development

ACTIVITY ONE

Next time you are with a friend, practise listening to them. Consciously decide, beforehand, that you are going to do less talking and more listening.

ACTIVITY TWO

Try to keep your 'attention out' for lengthy periods. Again, you must *choose* to do this, it won't just 'happen'.

ACTIVITY THREE

Notice your colleagues and identify the degree to which you do or do not think them to be good listeners. What is it about their *behaviour* that tells you that they do or do not listen?.

Using the Skills: Spotting the Problems

Read through the following conversation. Try to identify in what ways the health care worker could have *listened* more carefully. Note, too, when her own values and interpretations become evident. To what degree do they affect the conversation?

'How are you this morning'
'I'm fine. . .'
'You don't look it. You look as though you've had a rough night.'
'No. I think I'm OK. I'm still a bit worried about things.'
'Yes, I thought you were. You must try to stop worrying, though I know that's easier said than done. It doesn't get you anywhere in the end, though, does it?'
'No. I'm not really worrying a lot, though. I feel much better than I did. It's just. . .'
'You are getting all het up again. Try taking some deep breaths. You know that works for you'
'Yes. It's Alan. I wonder if he will cope whilst I'm away. He's never had me away from home before.'
'He's old enough, now, though, isn't he? He's 17. You've got to let go, sometime, haven't you?'
'I know. I just worry, that's all. I suppose its only natural.'
'Of course it is. But don't let it get out of proportion, that's all.'
'No. Thank you.'

Communications Skills Questionnaire: Listening to people

Read through the items in the following questionnaire and tick the response that corresponds to how you feel about the statement. If you are working in a group, you may want to compare your responses to the statements. There are no right or wrong answers but the statements can help you to clarify your own thinking and beliefs about the topic.

1. It is important to keep your attention focused on the other person when you are listening to them.

Strongly agree	Agree	Don't know	Disagree	Strongly disagree

2. I am quite good at keeping my attention 'out'.

Strongly agree	Agree	Don't know	Disagree	Strongly disagree

3. It is important to *show* that you are listening to the other person.

Strongly agree	Agree	Don't know	Disagree	Strongly disagree

4. It is vital to sit opposite someone when you are listening to them.

Strongly agree	Agree	Don't know	Disagree	Strongly disagree

5. Most of my colleagues are good listeners.

Strongly agree	Agree	Don't know	Disagree	Strongly disagree

6. I need to improve my listening skills

Strongly agree	Agree	Don't know	Disagree	Strongly disagree

7. Good listeners are born not made.

Strongly agree	Agree	Don't know	Disagree	Strongly disagree

8. Most people talk to much anyway.

Strongly agree	Agree	Don't know	Disagree	Strongly disagree

9. Talking things through is therapeutic for most people.

Strongly agree	Agree	Don't know	Disagree	Strongly disagree

10. I would like to be a better listener.

Strongly agree	Agree	Don't know	Disagree	Strongly disagree

Further Reading

Cox, M. 1978 *Structuring the Therapeutic Process*. Pergamon, London.

Egan, G. 1990 *The Skilled Helper*, 4th edn. Brooks/Cole, Pacific Grove, California.

Ernst, S. and Goodison, C. 1981 *In Your Own Hands: A Book of Self-Help Therapy*. Womens Press, London.

Morris, D. 1978 *Manwatching*. Triad/Panther, St Albans.

4
Talking to Clients

Keywords

● talking

● clients

● therapeutic interventions

● values.

The last chapter discussed the processes involved in listening to other people. As we noted in a previous chapter, many people feel that *talking* is easy. When we think a little more about it, though, it becomes evident that certain aspects of talking are not all that easy. Consider, for example, the following situations:

● A middle-aged man asks you what he should do about his marriage, which is breaking up.
● A young girl is very upset and begins to cry uncontrollably.
● An elderly person begins to tell you very personal things about her life.
● A colleague lacks confidence and doubts whether he will be able to stay in the job.

In each of these cases, the question is the same: what should you do? In this chapter, we discuss some of the options that are open to you when you are talking to clients and colleagues. Underpinning all this, though, is the essential skill of listening. As we have noted, listening is the primary skill in being helpful to other people. All of the other skills of communicating are secondary to it.

Talking to Clients

It is possible to divide up the sorts of skills used in talking to other people into the following categories:

● giving information
● supporting
● drawing out
● confronting
● coping with emotions.

This set of categories forms the basis of the discussion in this chapter. If you can become effective in each of these categories, you are well on the way to becoming an effective verbal communicator.

Giving information

We often have to give other people information. If someone asks us for directions, we give information. If someone asks us when they can see the doctor, we give information. If someone asks us when they will feel less depressed, we give information.

But stop! The last one is clearly inaccurate. Already, it would seem, there are times when it is fine to give information and times when it is not. Consider the following list of situations and decide when you *would* and when you *would not* give information. Then try to work out what are the common factors involved that make situations either those in which you do or do not give information:

● A client wants to know whether or not she should increase the dose of her insulin.
● A colleague asks you if it is legal to smoke at 15.
● A friend asks you if he should give up his girlfriend.
● A client asks you if he can see the occupational therapist.
● A visitor asks you about the visiting times.
● A person rings up to ask about the progress of one of your clients.
● A client asks you if she should kill herself.

How did you get on? What were the factors that made you decide whether or not you would or would not give information? There are, of course, many factors and, often, a decision to give information depends upon the *context* of the conversation. In other words the decision depends on:

● How well you know the other person.
● Your relationship with the other person.
● Your role in the organisation.
● Your knowledge base.
● The phsyical and psychological status of the person seeking the information.
● The question of confidentiality.

These are some of the issues, but there are others. One easy way to consider whether or not you should offer other people information is to think about what sort of information is being sought. Information can be roughly divided into two:

● **'Public' information** — examples, here, would be visiting times, times that the doctor visits the unit, shop opening hours and so forth. Generally speaking, public knowledge can be shared freely with others.
● **'Private' information** — this can take two forms. There is private information that various health care workers share about another person. Examples here would be a person's medical history, their blood pressure, their family status and so forth. Then there is another sort of 'private' information. This is information that a person has about him- or herself and shares only with a few other people, if at all. Think, for example, about things that you know about yourself that you do not readily tell other people. Now think about things that you *never* share with others. Such information cannot be freely given to others. Also in this category are topics about which it is *impossible* to give information. For example, I could never give you 'information' about what you should do about your boy or girlfriend. Nor could I give you 'information' about whether or not to leave home.

Given these two distinctions, it is important to distinguish between what really is 'information' and what is opinion or judgement. Thus, it is reasonable for me to give you information about the local social services department but it is not reasonable for me to give you information about what you should do about your marriage. This process of clarification can lead to some basic principles about information giving:

● Information should only be given if it is *right* to give it. Usually, this means that it is 'public' information.
● Information should be accurate.

● Information should not be confused with opinion and judgement. If someone asks for your opinion, that is one thing. To offer your opinion as if it were information, is quite another.

Supporting

Someone once described health care workers as 'compulsive carers'. It has been suggested that some people care for others as a way of making up for the care that they have not had themselves. No doubt we care for others for all sorts of reasons and with all sorts of motives. What is important, though, is that we offer appropriate support when it is called for. What sort of support, for instance, would you offer in the following situations?

● A 13-year-old girl asks if she can talk to you for the rest of the afternoon.
● An elderly man says that he cannot feed himself and would you help him.
● A young woman says that she feels suicidal and asks for your help.
● A colleague talks of dieting and wonders if you would help him.

Again, what do you do? How much support do you give and what determines how you make your decision? Much will depend on your beliefs about other people. Do you, for example, believe that other people should stand on their own two feet and fend for themselves? Do you feel that other people should be as autonomous as possible for as long as possible? Do you feel that we should all help each other as much as possible? Do you feel that we often have to be cruel to be kind to help others? Any of these beliefs will affect the degree of support that you offer to others. There are no easy answers in this field.

One thing, though, is clear. If you do offer support, make sure that it is *genuine*. In the end, you cannot feign interest, sympathy and support. You have to really feel it and really want to give it.

If you do commit yourself to supporting others, make sure that you can follow through your commitment. Make sure, too, that you avoid patronising, mothering or even smothering the other person. In the end, it is probably best to give minimal support and then to test the reaction. Often, people seem to thrive once they have been offered a little help. What is probably not a good idea is to try to take over the other person's life for them.

Whilst we can help others, it is important, too, that we stand back and let them help themselves wherever possible. All the time that we do things for others, we are stopping them from doing things for themselves. We are taking from them their independence. But there! My own values and beliefs are already creeping through. What is important right now is for you to discuss and clarify your own!

Drawing Out

If people are to work through their problems, they need to talk about them.

Unfortunately, it is not possible just to say 'What seems to be the problem?' and expect the other person to tell you. Very often, people do not know what is really worrying them until they have talked a little. It is here that the process of 'drawing out' is the skill that is required.

To draw someone out is to encourage them to talk, to help them to put into words some of the things that are currently something of a jumble. This process of verbalising is often therapeutic. There is an old saying that 'I don't know what I feel until I hear what I say'. This sums up the process of being drawn out exactly. What then are the specific skills of drawing out? They can be listed as follows:

- open questions
- reflection
- checking for understanding
- empathy building.

Open questions

Open questions are the sort that do not have a specific answer and to which the answer is never 'yes' or 'no'. They usually begin with the words 'what', 'why', 'where', 'when' or 'how'. Thus, all of the following are open questions:

- What are your feelings about that?
- How did you cope when that happened?
- Where did you go after that?

Note that you will never know what sort of answer to expect from asking an open question. Compare them, then, to *closed questions*. Closed questions usually evoke a single word or 'yes' or 'no' answer. All of the following are examples of closed questions:

- What is your name?
- Did you say that you have two children?
- Do you come to the clinic every week?

So far so good. The difference between open and closed questions is fairly clear, given these examples. Notice, though, that sometimes the issue is a little less clear cut. Consider the following examples. Which are they — open or closed?

- You didn't really mind moving, then?
- You're not very happy at the moment?

Both of these examples are, strictly speaking, closed questions that can be answered by 'yes' or 'no'. In reality, though, they are likely to be elaborated upon by the person who answers them. In the end, it seems likely that there is a range of questions that can be asked, ranging on the one hand from very open questions to, on the other hand, very closed questions.

If you are to become skilled in drawing out, the questions to aim at are the open ones, of all complexions. The effect of a series of open questions is not difficult to see. Nor is the effect of a series of closed questions.

In the following examples, the first health care worker uses closed questions; the second uses open questions. Notice the differences in how the conversations proceed and how, in the second example, the client is, indeed, drawn out by the other person.

Example one
  'Where were you living before you came to Birmingham?'
  'In Stoke.'
  'Did you like it there?'
  'No.'
  'Where did you live before that?'
  'Manchester.'
  'Did you prefer that?'
  'Not really, no.'

Example two
  'Can you tell me a little about where you lived in the past?'
  'Well, I lived in Brighton, on the south coast. Then I moved to Manchester and Stoke before I came to Birmingham . . . I liked it most of all in Brighton, although my husband wasn't particularly happy there . . . not really . . . he didn't settle. . .'
  'What happened in Brighton, then?'
  'Well, he was out of work for a long time. Then he was ill. It was a pity, really, because all the rest of us liked it there and he didn't. I suppose that's when all the problems really started. It all dated back to then.'

Clearly, in the first example, the conversation isn't going very far. The closed questions lead to monosyllabic answers. Note three things about the second example. First, the health care worker uses open questions. Second, they allow the other person plenty of time to talk and do not rush to fill in the gaps in the conversation. As a result, the talker continues to talk and continues to develop her end of the conversation: she is being drawn out. Third, it is the talker who does most of the talking. The person asking the open questions doesn't have to ask very many. And this is how it should be. Effective communication skills in a one-to-one relationship are dependent as much on the quality of listening as they are on a series of intervention strategies. When intervention strategies are used, the strategy of choice is the open question.

Reflection

There are two sorts of reflection. The first is where the listener simply echoes back to the talker the last words that were spoken. An example of this sort of reflection is:

'We continued to live in Brighton until things got really bad. My husband had been out of work for two years and was drinking heavily. Because of that, he felt that he was a burden to everyone. . .'

'He felt that he was a burden. . .'

'Well, he didn't like what was happening, put it like that. So we had to move. . .'

This is *straightforward reflection*. Sometimes (as in the above example) the actual words are reflected back. Sometimes, the listener paraphrases the last few words and echoes them back, as in the following example:

'It was a bit different in Manchester. John found work fairly quickly although it wasn't quite what he wanted. He wasn't very settled, even with a job. . .'

'He found a job but couldn't settle. . .'

'I suppose it was because of all those months in Brighton, without work and everything. No, he never did settle. . .'

Another sort of reflection is *selective reflection*. In this case, the listener echoes back the part of the last utterance that was emphasised in some way by the talker. The following is an example of the use of selective reflection:

'He stayed on in the job — he hated it though — but it was a job, at least. The main thing, it seemed to me, was that he was working. . .'

'He hated it, though. . .'

'He didn't like it at all. It really upset him. Nearly as much as not working at all.

Here, the listener has noted an emphasis on a group of almost 'throwaway' words and echoed them back once the speaker has paused. As a result, the speaker picks up on the issue and expands on it.

Both straightforward reflection and selective reflection are helpful strategies for helping another person to talk more about themselves. They do take practice. What you have to do, now, is to make a decision to use these types of reflection. Next time you are talking to a friend or client, try using reflection for at least part of the time. At first, you will feel slightly awkward and uncomfortable. As you discover how such methods really do help the other person, you will find them easier to use. The real point here is that you *must* undertake a conscious decision to use them. Merely reading about them will never make you skilled in their use. The skill comes from using them in real, live situations with real, live people. Use them today if you can.

Checking for understanding

This is what it says. You are listening to another person and you are not quite sure what they are saying, so you check. Such checking for understanding is often prefaced with words such as 'Can I just check what you meant just now. . . ?' Here is an example of checking for understanding in use:

'He was working for awhile. Then he was out again. He wasn't happy either way. He never really was happy. . .'
'Can I just check . . . you say he was working for awhile and then he was out of work again.'
'Yes, but he didn't like it either way. He wasn't happy when he was working and he wasn't happy when he wasn't. . . It was a horrible period, that. . .'

As people begin to disclose themselves to other people, their rate of talking often speeds up. Thoughts run into one another and are made into sentences. Sometimes, it is difficult for the listener to make sense of what is being said. It is at such points that checking for understanding techniques are most helpful. It is usually better to make sure that you are following the conversation and can make sense of it.

This is, of course, not always the case. Sometimes it is therapeutic for the talker merely to talk everything out in one go. Later, they can go back and pick out the pertinent points for further discussion. When this happens, all that is required of the listener is simply that they listen, without interrupting. As with most things, timing is all important here.

Empathy building

To empathise is to show that you understand the other person. Empathy has been variously described as 'standing in the other person's shoes' or 'entering the other person's frame of reference.'

We all look at the world slightly differently according to all sorts of life events and experiences. If, for example, I have had experience of other men being aggressive and threatening, I may come to see *all* men as aggressive and threatening. If, on the other hand, you have had pleasant experiences of men in general, you may find men agreeable.

The point for the health care worker is to try to appreciate how *this* person views people or the world in general. The next point is to express that empathy and that is done through empathy-building statements. These, as the name implies, are expressions that show that you are 'with' the other person and understanding their world view. Examples of such statements are:

'It sounds as though you were very angry when that happened. . .'
'It seems as though that made you fairly uncomfortable. . .'

Notice that empathy-building statements are always tentative in nature. The point about empathising is that it is a gradual process. We do not easily enter the world of another person. Therefore, it is better to proceed with caution and use expressions such as 'it sounds as though. . .' or 'it seems as if. . .', rather than using definite statements.

All of these interventions — open questions, reflections, checking for understanding and empathy-building statements — are means of helping the other person to talk things through. They form the basis of good communication skills and should be in every health care worker's repertoire of skills.

Confronting

For much of the time, drawing out interventions will be all that are needed to help another person talk through his or her problems. Sometimes, though, things get 'stuck'. Typically, one or more of the following things happen and a more confronting mode is called for:

- The client begins to repeat him- or herself and the conversation goes round in circles.
- The client constantly tells you how she sees herself in a totally negative light.
- There are discrepancies in what the client is telling you.

Depending on how well you know the client and depending on your relationship with him or her, you may feel it necessary to challenge what is being said. Some principles should be observed when challenging or confronting another person:

- Be very clear *what* you are confronting about.
- Only confront on one issue at a time.
- Do not turn the confrontaton into an opportunity to moralise or blame (e.g. 'I'm not surprised at what happened to you: you were being fairly stupid').
- Say what you have to say clearly and calmly and be prepared to repeat yourself, if necessary.

What follows is an example of confrontation in action. Note how the health care worker confronts and how she has to repeat what she says:

'No, he didn't ever seem to be happy. I wonder sometimes what *would* make him happy. . .'

'I notice that you don't talk about *your* feelings. What were *you* feeling all this time?'

'He should have settled down with the job . . . Manchester wasn't so bad really. . .'

'Yes, but what about *you*: what were *your* feelings?'

'Me? Oh . . . I didn't count. I wasn't *allowed* to have feelings. No one took any notice of me at all.'

Here, we notice that the first attempt at confrontation seems to go unnoticed. Sometimes, a person really does not hear the confrontation — perhaps because they do not want to hear it. However, when the listener gently repeats the confrontation, the client opens up her own feelings and begins to focus in on herself. Gentle confrontation, done well, can push a relationship along a little. However, it should never be done aggressively or for the sake of scoring points. Confrontation, in other words, should always be done supportively and with the aim of helping the client.

Coping with Emotions

Sometimes, as a person is talking, they may become upset and start to cry. What do you do? This is a question that worries a lot of people involved in caring for, and talking to, others. Sometimes, other people's tears cause us to remember our own, hidden, unhappiness. Sometimes, the crying reminds us of our own need to cry. Sometimes, though, we simply do not know what to do to help the other person.

The topic of helping people with their emotions deserves a book in itself — and many have been written about the nature of emotional release. Some psychologists believe that expressing emotion is a healthy sign. This seems often to be the case in someone who has been depressed. It seems that many depressed people bottle-up their emotions and end up turning hostile feelings against themselves — hence, the depressed feelings. Whatever the pros and cons of the therapeutic value or otherwise of emotional release, the following guidelines are offered, based on the literature on the topic, on research findings and on the author's experience as a counsellor:

- Emotional release is self-limiting. No one, it appears, ever failed to *stop* crying.
- Crying and emotional release seem to help more than they hinder.

Therefore, it seems to be a good idea to allow the person to cry rather than to encourage them to stop.

● It is important to see the difference between the client's emotional state and your own. If you find yourself becoming upset, that is to do with your own problems — not the client's. It is important to appreciate the difference and not to assume that you are both upset about the same thing. Try to keep your problems and your client's problems as two separate issues.

● Gentle touch on the part of the helper often conveys support beyond words. You do not have to talk when someone is crying. Merely offering them your hand to hold may be all the support they need. Whatever happens, try not to overtalk because you are unsure what to do.

● After someone has cried, they often want to sit quietly. In this phase, they are often piecing together new insights that are occurring to them, once the crying is over. Again, do not rush to fill this silence with your own words. The client is nearly always coping on his or her own. All you need to do is be there.

Helping people with their emotions is often difficult for people who are new to the health care field. Some health care workers never get to be very good at helping in this setting. The main thing is to do a little rather than to do a lot. You can help a great deal if you can allow the other person to express their feelings completely — even if this means sitting while the other person cries a considerable amount. If you can offer support in situations of this sort, you are already on the way to becoming a skilled and human carer.

Talking with Children

At first sight, it would seem likely that talking with children is much the same as talking with adults. However, some people are unsure how to talk to children and, as a result, either avoid them or talk down to them. The following issues are important in thinking about this important aspect of communication*:

● Find out what the child likes to be called. Do not assume that he or she will like you to call him by a nickname or a name used in the family.

● Be aware of levels and stages of child development. This can help you to pitch your questions and responses at the correct level.

● Respond to the individual child as an individual. Do not assume that 'all children are much the same'.

*I am indebted to my colleague and friend, Jim Richardson of the University of Wales College of Medicine for his help on this section.

● Talk to children 'normally': neither talk down to them nor patronise them and never call them 'dear' or 'love'.

● Respect the child. Remember that he or she is a human being just like you, only a little younger.

● Think about the environment in which you talk to the child. If you are working in a hospital or clinical setting, find a quiet room in which to talk.

● Use play to communicate with smaller children.

● Do not try to copy children's slang or adopt their mannerisms.

● Believe them. Trust must be the basis of any relationship and it is particularly important with children.

● Remember that most children are taught not to talk to strangers. Therefore, some children will prefer talking to you only in the company of one of their parents.

● Allow the child to determine the issue of proximity. Do not stand or sit too close to them or automatically put your arm around them. Allow the child to decide on these issues.

In this chapter, we have explored some of the main skills in talking on a one-to-one basis. I would say that these skills are the bedrock skills upon which all others are built. If you can become skilled in the methods described here and at the same time retain your own spontaneity and naturalness, then you have much to offer people who are suffering from emotional or life problems. Become good at these skills and the others will follow.

Communication Skills Check List

● Talking to clients involves a variety of skills.

● Open questions are generally more effective in drawing people out than are closed questions.

● Reflection is an effective way of encouraging people to talk.

● We need to check that we understand what we are hearing.

● Empathy building involves trying to understand the world as the other person sees it.

Activities for Skills Development

ACTIVITY ONE

Pay attention, this week, to the interventions you use when you are at work with clients. At this stage, merely *notice* what you say.

ACTIVITY TWO

Once you are familiar with observing yourself talking to others, attempt to use other sorts of interventions: particularly the drawing out sort.

ACTIVITY THREE

Observe your colleagues at work. Notice the sorts of interventions that they use and note down the ones that are most effective. Pay attention to the *language* that they use when talking to clients.

Using the Skills: Spotting the Problems

Read through the following conversation between health worker and client. Try to identify the ways in which the conversation is *not* particularly therapeutic. Then try to identify how some of the skills described in this chapter might have helped.

'I feel awful at the moment . . .'

'Do you? I suppose everybody does at this time of the year.'

'No. This is the anniversary of when my husband lost his job. He's been out of work a year now.'

'I expect he'll find another one. You mustn't worry so much.'

'I doubt it. He's 55 now and unskilled. There's not much chance of him finding anything now.'

'You look at things in a very negative way. He *might* find a job — especially if you are a bit more positive about it. It can't help him if you take that sort of approach.'

'No, I suppose not. I can't help it, though, I feel so miserable at the moment.'

'Don't cry. Here's a handkerchief. Blow your nose and stop crying. He *will* find a job. I know lots of people who have, even after a long time.'

'I'm sorry. I shouldn't bother you with my problems.'

'Don't be silly. That's what I'm here for.'

Communications Skills Questionnaire: Talking to clients

Read through the items in the following questionnaire and tick the response that corresponds to how you feel about the statement. If you are working in a group, you may want to compare your responses to the statements. There are no right or wrong answers but the statements can help you to clarify your own thinking and beliefs about the topic.

1. Talking is a natural process. I don't need any help with it.

Strongly agree	Agree	Don't know	Disagree	Strongly disagree

2. If we are to work as health care workers, we need to pay attention to what we do and say.

Strongly agree	Agree	Don't know	Disagree	Strongly disagree

3. Most health care workers are good at coping with other people's emotion.

Strongly agree	Agree	Don't know	Disagree	Strongly disagree

4. I'm not really sure what to do when someone starts crying.

Strongly agree	Agree	Don't know	Disagree	Strongly disagree

5. I could learn to draw people out a little more.

Strongly agree	Agree	Don't know	Disagree	Strongly disagree

6. Listening is more important than talking in a health care relationship.

Strongly agree	Agree	Don't know	Disagree	Strongly disagree

7. Most of my colleagues talk too much.

Strongly agree	Agree	Don't know	Disagree	Strongly disagree

8. The skilled colleagues are the ones who really listen to what people say.

Strongly agree	Agree	Don't know	Disagree	Strongly disagree

9. More interpersonal skills training should be included in school and college curricula.

Strongly agree	Agree	Don't know	Disagree	Strongly disagree

10. I want to concentrate on being more effective as a listener and talker.

Strongly agree	Agree	Don't know	Disagree	Strongly disagree

Further reading

Murgatroyd, S. 1986 *Counselling and Helping*. Methuen, London.

Murgatroyd, S. and Woolfe, R. 1982 *Coping with Crisis: Understanding and Helping People in Need*. Harper and Row, London.

5

One-to-one Communication: The therapeutic conversation

Keywords

- opening
- developing
- structuring
- ending.

We all talk to each other. The point about therapeutic conversations with clients, though, is that they are just that: therapeutic. In other words, they are for the benefit of the client and their aim is to help. In this sense, therapeutic conversations are different to other sorts: they are generally more focused and their structure needs to be thought about.

In this chapter, we go through the various stages of a therapeutic conversation. This is not to suggest that this chapter will make you into a counsellor or therapist — far from it. Such skills need to be developed through detailed training and over a fairly lengthy period of time. However, we can all get better at being therapeutic through fairly ordinary conversations.

So what does distinguish a therapeutic conversation from any other sort? The features that make them different are:

- A therapeutic conversation is 'client-centred': it is concerned with the problems of the client not those of the other person.
- A therapeutic conversation is one that makes the client feel better in some way.
- A therapeutic conversation is one that the health care worker structures to make it more helpful to the client.

In an ordinary conversation, the talk goes back and forward between the two people with little focus and with attention shared between the two parties. The following two examples make clear some of these distinctions.

Example one: an 'ordinary' conversation
'How are you doing?'
'I'm OK. How about you?'
'Fine. Did you go out last night?'
'Yes. We went to the pub — the one at the top of the hill, just outside the town. I can't remember the name.'
'It's the Barge and Anchor, I think'
'That's it. It's quite good in there. There were lots of people there last night. We all got a bit drunk.'
'We went to the pictures. Me and Jane. It was OK. I'm never sure whether I like the pictures or not, really. I mean, you can always get videos, can't you?'
'What did you see? Anything good?'

Example two: a 'therapeutic' conversation
'Hello. How are you feeling today?'
'I'm more settled, I think. How about you?'
'I'm fine. Did you sleep well?'
'Yes. Very. I'm sleeping much better now and that makes me more relaxed. I think I need to sleep quite a lot at the moment.'
'And it makes you feel better . . .'
'Well, it seems to. There was a time when I hardly slept at all. I used to come in late, drink a lot of coffee and then have difficulty in getting off at all.'
'And you found you were more "wound up" then?'
'Definitely. I've stopped drinking coffee altogether now and I get to bed at a reasonable time. It all helps.'

'What else is making you feel better?'
'Oh. Lots of things. The staff, I think. I find talking about things helps a lot.'

In the first example, the conversation was shared between the two people concerned, as is appropriate between two friends. In the second example, the conversation is focused much more on the client than on the helper — although the helper is quite prepared to mention how she feels as well.

Holding a therapeutic conversation means paying attention to what happens as a conversation develops. It has to have structure and it means that the carer has to think about what she or he says and does. First of all, though, the conversation has to start.

Opening a Conversation

How do *you* start a conversation? Do you know? If you have never thought about it, it probably sounds like an odd sort of question. Think about the following 'starters'. Which, if any, are the sorts of ways that *you* start talking to other people, and particularly, clients:

● 'Hello, how are you?'
● 'Hi!'
● 'Hello, are you all right?'
● 'Hello, nice to see you.'

Think about these starters. What is the difference between them? One clear difference is that some really do tend to start a conversation whilst the others tend only to be a passing acknowledgement. If you only ever make acknowledgements, you leave the conversation starting up to the other person.

In a therapeutic conversation, the onus is usually on *you* to start it. Sit and think about ways that you could improve the way you start talking to clients. Note, too, what you *call* the other person. Do you automatically call them by their first name? their full name? or do you ever call them 'dear' or 'love'? Whilst the latter are common forms of greetings between friends and family members, they are probably best avoided in therapeutic conversations. They suggest a certain 'matiness' or they may be construed as patronage. On the whole, they are best avoided.

Developing a Conversation

Once you have started the conversation, how do you develop it? The point, in the therapeutic conversation, is to keep the conversation largely focused on the other person. It is here that the 'drawing out' skills that were discussed in a previous chapter come to the fore.

If you can use open questions, reflections, checking for understanding and empathy-building statements, you are well on the way to developing a therapeutic conversation. Consider using, also, 'minimal prompts'. These are small nudges in the conversation that encourage the other person to continue talking. Example of minimal prompts include:

- 'mm'
- 'Yes'
- 'Go on'
- 'What happened next?'
- 'I'm with you' and so on.

Also, it is possible to offer non-verbal prompts through smiling and nodding the head. Use these prompts wisely and thoughtfully though, there is nothing worse than the person who grins inanely all the time the other person is talking and who grunts and nods at the same time!

Remember, try to keep the conversation on the other person. Be honest and open in your replies to questions from the client but always be prepared to return to *their* perspective and *their* life situation. Try, as far as possible to enter their 'frame of reference' — their way of viewing the world. This means that you have to avoid being judgemental and avoid disagreeing with their point of view. At base, it means openly accepting what the other person says without any attempt at censure — not always easy.

Finally, in this section, it is useful to note how deep a conversation is getting. A useful gauge is offered in Figure 5.1. It indicates three levels of depth in a therapeutic conversation. At the first level, only 'safe' things are talked about. As the conversation progresses and trust develops, the client discloses more and the conversation becomes deeper. It is likely that many conversations never go deeper than this level. Level three, the deepest level of

Levels in a Therapeutic Conversation
Level one. The superficial level. Conversation at this level is polite and safe.
Level two. The deeper level. Conversation at this level tends to focus on more personal issues and on feelings.
Level three. The deepest level. Conversation covers the person's deepest fears and anxieties. Issues such as meaning, sexuality and personal identity may be discussed here.

Figure 5.1 Levels in therapeutic conversation.

all is the level at which *anything* is talked about, and at which the client will talk about his or her most intimate thoughts.

Working through these levels takes time and the process cannot be rushed. You cannot force someone to disclose things that they are not happy to. Nor should you attempt to. It is far more therapeutic if people disclose things gently and slowly. If they *do* disclose a lot in a short space of time, they often find themselves embarrassed and sometimes never return to a conversation at that depth. It is almost as if they have seen what is possible and have been frightened of what they have seen. Generally speaking, a conversation will only develop to level three when trust is at its highest and when both parties have got to know each other very well. Usually, the listener has given out 'signals' that he or she can cope with level three disclosures, before they are made. Level three disclosures more often happen in counselling and psychotherapy than they do in therapeutic conversations.

Structuring a Conversation

Minimal structuring can help the conversation. First, it is useful if you make it clear at the beginning, how long you will be able to spend with the client. Thus, it is not unreasonable to say 'I have half an hour and I would quite like to sit down and talk to you, if you would like that. . .' Often, people do not disclose what they are really worrying about until near the end of the conversation.

If the person knows when the end is likely to come, it gives him or her the opportunity to talk about the particular worry. If the conversation ends rather abruptly the client may feel distressed at not having been able to express all that they wanted to.

To this end, too, it helps if you remind the client when the conversation is going to end. Thus, it helps to say: 'We've got five more minutes . . . is there anything else you wanted to talk about?' Read on a page, like this, these statements may sound odd. Try them! They really do work and they help the client to work through problems in a conversation in a way that they would not otherwise be able to do.

Ending a Conversation

'Getting away' from the other person is sometimes a problem. Again, if you have already indicated how long the conversation is going to last, it will not be such a problem. Remember, though, the point made in the last section: people often talk about what is *really* worrying them towards the end of a conversation. They may, therefore, be in full flight when it is time to stop.

Again, expressions such as the following can be useful here: 'I sense that there is a lot more to talk about and I would like us to meet again tomorrow.' This can be followed up with the statement: 'We will have to stop, now, but we will talk again tomorrow.' Clearly, you will have to 'find your own words' to say these things but they often need to be said. If you *do* make the offer of a further conversation, make sure that you can stick to it and that you do meet again the next day.

Once this sort of conversation and this sort of structured relationship has started, it is usually much easier to carry on subsequent occasions. Ironically, it seems that structure also brings a certain freedom. Once the structure has been established in the conversation, the client is free to talk about anything.

Think for a while about how you end conversations. Are you, for example, a person who begins to back away in the effort to end? Or do you end in mid-sentence and merely say goodbye? Spend some time rehearsing ways of finishing conversations. If necessary, role-play 'endings' with colleagues or friends. We all need all the help we can get in these matters.

Communication Skills Check List

● A therapeutic conversation is not a form of counselling but a means of helping clients to talk more about themselves.

● Opening and closing conversations are important and sometimes difficult aspects of communication.

● It is important to structure conversations if they are to be effective.

Activities for Skills Development

ACTIVITY ONE

Listen to someone you consider to be an 'expert' in talking with clients. Note their behaviour and what it is that they say. Notice, particularly, how they structure and end the conversation.

ACTIVITY TWO

Make a sustained effort to structure the next conversation that you have with a client, along the lines suggested in this chapter. Do not be too hard on yourself, though, and allow yourself to make mistakes.

ACTIVITY THREE

Undertake to make a contract with yourself that you will work on your conversations with clients. You may not want to follow all of the guidelines suggested here but try to introduce a pattern of working with clients in a therapeutic way.

Using the Skills: Spotting the Problems

Read through the following conversation between a health care worker and a client. It contains examples of both good and bad practice. Try to identify both aspects and suggest ways that the conversation could be improved upon.

'Hello, Mrs Jenkins, I thought that I would come and talk to you for ten minutes.'

'Hello, Rebecca. It's nice to see you again. What have you been up to?'

'Oh, lots of things. I've been out with my boyfriend last night. We're thinking of getting engaged and everything. It's quite a busy time at the moment. My mum's pleased though: I think she likes him, really.'

'She'll miss you when you leave home, though. . .'

'I suppose so. Still . . . it has to happen some time. How is *your* daughter? Have you seen her lately?'

'Yes, she came in yesterday. . .'

'And. . . ?'

'We still find it difficult to talk.'

'What happens?'

'Well, we start off all right. She tells me what she's been doing and I tell her what I've been up to. Then we just start to argue.'

'What do you argue about?'

'My being in here, mostly.'

'What happens?'

'She thinks I should be able to manage on my own. She doesn't really understand what is wrong with me.'

'My mum's a bit like that. She never really understands what happens to me.'

'She *tries* to understand but I think she thinks I put it all on.'

'What do you do, then. . . ?'

'I get mad at her! I usually start shouting at her and then we end up really arguing. It never seems to get any better.'

'What needs to happen then?'

'We both need to calm down, I suppose.'

'Can you do that?'

(Laughs) 'That's a good question! I hope so. . .'

'It might help . . . mightn't it. . . ?'

'Yes. I'll have to go . . . Thanks. . .'

'OK. Shall we talk a bit more tomorrow?'

'Yes, I'd like that. You seem to understand what I'm on about . . . see you tomorrow.'

'Bye.'

'Bye, love.'

Communications Skills Questionnaire: One-to-one communication

Read through the items in the following questionnaire and tick the response that corresponds to how you feel about the statement. If you are working in a group, you may want to compare your responses to the statements. There are no right or wrong answers but the statements can help you to clarify your own thinking and beliefs about the topic.

1. The idea of a therapeutic conversation is too complicated. I just talk to people.

Strongly agree	Agree	Don't know	Disagree	Strongly disagree

2. Many of the conversations I have with clients aren't particularly therapeutic.

Strongly agree	Agree	Don't know	Disagree	Strongly disagree

3. I need to work on starting conversations.

Strongly agree	Agree	Don't know	Disagree	Strongly disagree

4. Some of my colleagues are very effective at using therapeutic conversation.

Strongly agree	Agree	Don't know	Disagree	Strongly disagree

5. Most people in the health care field need to improve their conversational skills.

Strongly agree	Agree	Don't know	Disagree	Strongly disagree

6. Its no good reading about it: you have to *do* it!

Strongly agree	Agree	Don't know	Disagree	Strongly disagree

7. I would like to develop more structure in my conversations.

Strongly agree	Agree	Don't know	Disagree	Strongly disagree

8. I am quite good at ending conversations.

Strongly agree	Agree	Don't know	Disagree	Strongly disagree

9. My conversations just seem to drift along without any real point.

Strongly agree	Agree	Don't know	Disagree	Strongly disagree

10. Sometimes I find it difficult to think what to say next.

Strongly agree	Agree	Don't know	Disagree	Strongly disagree

Further Reading

Baruth, L.G. 1987 *An Introduction to the Counselling Profession.* Prentice Hall, Englewood Cliffs, New Jersey.

Bolger, A.W. (ed) 1982 *Counselling in Britain: A Reader.* Batsford Academic, London.

Rogers, C.R. 1967 *On Becoming a Person.* Constable, London.

6
Group Communication

Keywords

- types of groups
- groups in the health care field
- advantages and disadvantages
- group facilitation.

We all live and work in a variety of groups. Some are naturally occurring groups: our family group, for example. Some are set up for a particular purpose. Some groups, as we shall see, never meet. In this chapter we explore aspects of groups and group life and consider how communication can be improved in group work.

Types of Groups

A distinction can be made between two sorts of groups: primary and secondary groups. A primary group is a face-to-face group where all members of the group get to know each other. Examples of primary groups include:

- therapy groups
- relatives' meetings

- the nuclear family
- committee meetings.

Secondary groups, on the other hand, are much more widely distributed and members may not get to know each other. Examples of secondary groups are:

- the members of a trade union
- the citizens of a state
- a professional group, such as health visitors.

In both sorts of groups, different norms and different dynamics occur. Whilst both groups have sets of rules by which members are controlled and organised, these are much more evident in primary groups. It is primary groups that we will concentrate on in this chapter.

One thing that is immediately noticeable about people in small groups (and probably in large ones, too) is that *their behaviour is different when they are in a group when compared to when they are not in the group.* You may have noticed, for instance, that some of your colleagues are quite different when they are in a meeting.

You may find that clients act differently on a one-to-one basis when compared to how they act in groups. The point about groups is that people have to make compromises. There is always a tension in a group between the needs of the group and the needs of the individual.

Whilst we can mostly do what we like when we are on our own, when we are with a group of other people, we have to make allowances and concessions. To bear this in mind is a useful starting point for understanding communication in groups.

Groups in the Health Care Field

The caring and health care workers organise and run many sorts of groups from educational and support groups to committees and management groups. These are some of the sorts of groups that you may come across in your work:

- the organisational group: colleagues and co-workers
- support groups
- therapy groups
- relaxation groups
- counselling groups
- committee meetings
- unit meetings
- learning and teaching groups

- quality circles
- case conferences
- management groups
- conferences.

If you are not familiar with any of these sorts of groups, try to find out whether or not they are run within your organisation and try to find out as much as you can about the structure and function of them.

Reasons for Running Groups

Try to think of other advantages of working in groups. Also consider whether or not there are different advantages to different sorts of groups. For example, are committees similar in their advantages to therapy groups?

Advantages of Groups

A lot can be achieved in a group that cannot be achieved between individuals. Whilst, as we have seen, people always have to compromise, to some degree, when they become group members, the advantages probably outweigh the disadvantages. Here are some advantages of working in groups:

- Decision-making can be shared.
- People can compare and contrast their experiences.
- More people can be involved in the decision-making process than is possible on a one-to-one basis.
- A sense of community can be generated by a group.
- A feeling of purpose and enterprise can be achieved within a group setting.
- Some people prefer working in groups.
- Expertise can be shared.
- Learning from other people can occur.
- They are economical in terms of peoples' time and the cost involved.
- They allow people to develop coping strategies.
- They mirror 'real life'.

Disadvantages of Groups

There are disadvantages, too, in working in groups. Some of these can be identified as follows:

- Not everyone gets heard in a group.
- Some people don't like groups.
- Minority views may not get supported.

- Groups may lose direction and become 'stale'.
- Consensus decision-making may be the *only* sort that occurs in some groups.

Try to identify the disadvantages that you see in the groups that work in your organisation.

Group Development

Groups of whatever sort tend to develop in characteristic ways. These are identified in Figure 6.1. A typical group starts off slowly, with all group members being on their best behaviour and eager to please. As the group develops, there is a tension between the needs of individuals and the needs of the group. It is at this point that people have to learn to compromise if the group is to survive.

Stages of Group Development
Stage one. Introductory stage: people are polite to each other and take time to get to know one another.
Stage two. Conflict stage: people start to fall out with one another as they seek a compromise between their own needs and the needs of the group.
Stage three. Negotiation stage: the group forms unwritten rules or norms about procedure.
Stage four. Working stage: the group works together having sorted out individual differences.

Figure 6.1 Stages in group development.

In the next stage, the group members develop unspoken 'norms' about what can and can't be done and what can and can't be talked about. Finally, the group works together as a harmonious whole. Think about groups that you meet with regularly and see to what degree you found the group to work through these sorts of stages.

Being a Group Member

Not everyone likes being in groups. Some people find the prospect of facing a roomful of other people threatening. This can cause us to *regress* or to return to a mode of behaviour that worked for us in the past. Put simply, we become a bit childish when we are threatened. We may show this in a number of ways in a group.

First, we may become very quiet and refuse to say anything. Alternatively we may chat to the person sitting next to us in a low voice. This is known as 'pairing'. Again, we may become very negative and try to 'wreck' the group. As health care workers it is important that we remain as positive and as useful as possible during the life of a group that we are a member of. Try to notice, first, other people's behaviour in groups. Then begin to notice your own and ask yourself how you could add to the work of the group.

It is possible to identify the qualities and skills of a good effective group member from reading the literature and research on the topic. The effective group member will:

- contribute, verbally, to the life of the group
- listen to other group members when they speak
- take direction from the group leader or facilitator
- be prepared to self-disclose
- keep to the topic in hand
- be positive in his or her contributions
- avoid being late coming to the group
- avoid leaving until the group meeting has finished.

Running Groups

You might be asked to run a group. If you are, it is helpful if you know the sorts of things that make a group run smoothly. We have discussed some of the advantages and disadvantages of group work and these give some clue to possible problems. The rule that applies here is that the more *structure* that can be introduced (at least initially) the more likely the group is to proceed. The important questions to ask *before* you set up a group are these:

- What *exactly* is the purpose of the group? What will people coming to the group expect of it? What are the aims of the group?
- How many people will be in the group?
- Where will the group meeting be held? Will it always be held there or will the location change?
- For how long will the group meeting run?
- At what time and on what date will it meet?
- Have all group members had sufficient time to make arrangements for attendance?

- Are all participants *willing* participants. One way to ensure that a group does not function is to force people to attend!
- What else do I need to know about the proposed group?

With the answers to these questions, it is then possible to start planning the group meeting. Whatever the function of the group (unless it is a formal committee meeting), the following stages can be worked through:

- Start promptly and spell out the aims of the group meeting.
- Introduce yourself and then invite each person in turn, around the group, to introduce themselves and to say a few things about themselves.
- If there is a programme or an agenda, work through it item by item.
- If there is no agenda, invite topics for discussion, bearing in mind the overall aims of the meeting.
- As the group develops, ask questions yourself to clarify, to encourage other points of view to help quieter members of the group to be heard.
- Towards the end of the group meeting, invite each person, in turn, to say: (i) what they least liked about the meeting; and then (ii) what they most liked about the meeting. Take a note of these points for consideration for the next meeting.

After your first meeting, it is helpful to review what you did as a group facilitator. Here, the following questions can be helpful in evaluating the meeting and in planning the next:

- Were the aims of the meeting achieved?
- Did everyone have a chance to introduce themselves properly?
- Did everyone speak at least once during the meeting? If not, did everyone who *wanted* to speak get the chance?
- Did anyone dominate the proceedings? If so, what can be done about this next time?
- What were the points raised during the 'least liked' and 'most liked' rounds? How can they be incorporated into the next meeting?

Group facilitation is, for some people, a painful business. Other people enjoy it very much. It is particularly useful, if you have had little experience of group facilitation, to base your style on that of someone you have seen at work and who is successful.

If, at first, you copy that person, after a while, and as your confidence grows, you will develop your own style. Make sure, too, that you read up on the sorts of activities and exercises that can be used in groups. The further reading section towards the end of this chapter lists books that contain exercises of this sort.

Communication Skills Check List

- Groups can be primary or secondary.
- If small groups are to run effectively, they need to be structured.
- As groups develop, the structure becomes less important.
- There are advantages and disadvantages to working in groups.
- Planning is essential if you are asked to run a group yourself.

Activities for Skills Development

ACTIVITY ONE

Next time you are in a group meeting, simply observe what goes on.

ACTIVITY TWO

Next, make a conscious effort to say something in the next meeting and notice how other people in the group respond to what you have to say.

ACTIVITY THREE

Ask permission to keep a simple sociogram in a group meeting. This means that you note down who makes verbal interventions and to whom and also, how often various people make verbal interventions. Note, afterwards, who talks most and least. Note, too, who gets talked *to* most in the group.

Using the Skills: Spotting the Problems

Read through the following two examples of groups at work and try to identify the developmental stages that they are at. How could the facilitator help each group to develop further?

Example one

'Does anyone know why we are here?'

'If you listened a little more, you would have heard David talking about what the group was for.'

'I think you should leave each other alone. You two always seem to fall out. You both did last week and it doesn't help the rest of us who are supposed to benefit from this group.'

'I propose that we move on. This is getting very boring.'

'What will we do if we "move on" as you put it? This group seems to be going nowhere. I'm not sure I'm getting anything out of it at all.'

'That's because you only think of yourself.'

'Well, I came here for some help. A fat lot of help I'm getting, too.'

Example two

'It might be useful if we all said a few words about our backgrounds. . .'

(Silence)

'Jane, would you like to tell the group a little bit about yourself?'

'I'm Jane and I come from London. I'm hoping that the group might help me with my confidence.'

'Thank you, Jane . . . what about other people. . . ? David?'

'I'm David and I'm . . . mm . . . I'm not sure why I'm here!'

(Laughter)

'I'm Sarah and I feel a bit uncomfortable at the moment. I came from Bristol and I work as a typist there. . .'

Communications Skills Questionnaire: Group communication

Read through the items in the following questionnaire and tick the response that corresponds to how you feel about the statement. If you are working in a group, you may want to compare your responses to the statements. There are no right or wrong answers but the statements can help you to clarify your own thinking and beliefs about the topic.

1. I am nervous of groups.

Strongly agree	Agree	Don't know	Disagree	Strongly disagree

2. Other colleagues are much more effective in groups than I am.

Strongly agree	Agree	Don't know	Disagree	Strongly disagree

3. I have had a lot of experience of being in groups.

Strongly agree	Agree	Don't know	Disagree	Strongly disagree

4. I will make a conscious effort to notice group behaviour in future.

Strongly agree	Agree	Don't know	Disagree	Strongly disagree

5. The best way to learn about groups is by being a group member.

Strongly agree	Agree	Don't know	Disagree	Strongly disagree

6. I would like to lead a group meeting.

Strongly agree	Agree	Don't know	Disagree	Strongly disagree

7. I intend to read more about group facilitation.

Strongly agree	Agree	Don't know	Disagree	Strongly disagree

8. All health care workers need to be effective group members.

Strongly agree	Agree	Don't know	Disagree	Strongly disagree

9. Groups do not suit everyone.

Strongly agree	Agree	Don't know	Disagree	Strongly disagree

10. All groups are similar in some ways.

Strongly agree	Agree	Don't know	Disagree	Strongly disagree

Further Reading

Burnard, P. 1990 *Learning Human Skills: An Experiential Guide for Nurses,* 2nd edn. Heinemann, Oxford.

Burnard, P. 1989 *Teaching Interpersonal Skills: An Experiential Handbook for Health Professionals.* Chapman and Hall, London.

Whitaker, D.S. 1987 *Using Groups to Help People.* Tavistock/Routledge, London.

7
Being Assertive

Keywords

●   assertion

●   aggression

●   submission.

What is Assertion?

We have noted that both caring and working in organisations take their toll on the individual. Sometimes the person's own needs become lost beneath the demands of the organisation or profession. One positive way of coping with stress in organisations and in the health care field is to become more assertive.

Assertiveness is often confused with being aggressive, but there are important differences. An assertive person is one who can state clearly and calmly what they want to say, does not back down in the face of disagreement and is prepared to repeat what they have to say, if necessary. The following are some of the barriers to assertiveness:

●   **Lack of practice** — you do not test your limits enough and discover whether you can be more assertive.
●   **Being unclear about what you want** — you do not have clear standards

and you are unsure of what you want.

- **Fear of other people's hostility** — you are afraid of anger or negative responses and you want to be considered reasonable.
- **Undervaluing yourself** — you do not feel that you have the right to stand firm and demand correct and fair treatment.
- **Poor presentation** — your self-expression tends to be vague, unimpressive, confusing or emotional.

Given that most health care workers spend much of their time considering the needs of others, it seems likely that many overlook the personal needs identified within this list of barriers to assertiveness. Part of the process of coping with stress is also the process of learning to identify and assert personal needs and wants.

A continuum that accounts for a range of types of behaviour, ranging from the submissive to the aggressive, with assertive behaviour being the mid point may be drawn, (Figure 7.1.)

Submissive Approach: (pussyfooting)	Assertive Approach	Aggressive Approach: (sledgehammering)
The person avoids conflict and confrontation by avoiding the topic in hand.	The person is clear, calm and prepared to repeat what she has to say.	The person is heavy-handed and makes a personal attack of the issue.

Figure 7.1 Three possible approaches to confrontation.

It has been suggested that we feel anxiety at the prospect of confronting another person. As a result of this anxiety we tend to either 'pussyfoot' (and be submissive) or 'sledgehammer' (and be aggressive). So it is with being assertive. Most people, when they are learning how to assert themselves experience anxiety and, as a result, tend to be either submissive or aggressive.

Other people handle that anxiety by swinging right the way through the continuum. They start submissively, then develop a sort of confidence and rush into an aggressive attack on another person. Alternatively, other people deal with their anxiety by starting an encounter very aggressively and quickly back off into submission. The level and calm approach of being assertive takes practice, nerve and confidence.

Consider the following examples of the three types:

Example 1: the pussyfooting approach
'There's something I want to talk to you about . . . I don't really know how

to put this . . . whatever you do, don't take offence at what I have to say. . .'

'I don't expect you will like this but I think it is better that I say it than keep quiet about it . . . on the other hand, perhaps it's better to say nothing.'

'I know that you have an awful lot of work and I don't want to add to it. Perhaps I ought to discuss what I have in mind with someone else.'

Example 2: the sledgehammer approach
'What you do annoys me. If you had any feelings at all, you wouldn't get home so late . . . but that's typical of you.'

'I give up with you. I bet you don't even know what I'm upset about. . .'

'Everybody round here is busy. I don't know why you think you're so special. I want you to take on another caseload.'

The Assertive Approach
'I would prefer it if you could get home a little earlier.'

'I'm feeling angry at the moment and I want to discuss our relationship.'

'I would like you to consider taking on Mrs Jones and her family.'

Notice, too, in your own behaviour and that of others, that posture and 'body language' often have much to do with the degree to which a statement is perceived by others as submissive, aggressive or assertive. These types of postures and body statements may be described using the three approaches, thus:

The Pussyfooting Approach
● hunched or rounded shoulders
● failure to face the other person directly
● eye contact averted
● nervous smile
● fiddling with hands
● nervous gestures
● voice low-pitched and apologetic.

The Sledgehammer Approach
● hands on hips or arms folded
● very direct eye contact
● angry expression
● loud voice
● voice threatening or angry
● threatening or provocative hand gestures.

The Assertive Approach

- face-to-face with the other person
- 'comfortable' eye contact
- facial expression that is 'congruent' with what is being said
- voice clear and calm.

What is notable from these descriptions of three different approaches to confrontation is that the pussyfooting and sledgehammer approaches can have physical as well as psychological effects. The person who frequently adopts one of these two approaches in their dealings with others will often find that they are both physically and emotionally stressed by the experience.

Becoming assertive is a potent method of learning to cope with all aspects of personal stress. It can also help to overcome organisational stress, in that the assertive person is rather more likely to express their own needs and wants and is more likely to be heard.

Why be Assertive?

Examples of how assertiveness can be useful include the following situations:

- When used to express the idea that a person is being asked to do too much by their employer.
- When used by a person who has never been able to express their wants and needs in a marriage.
- When used by the health care worker when facing bureaucratic processes in trying to get help for a client.
- In everyday situations in shops, offices, restaurants and other places where a stated service being offered is not actually being given.
- When used by the health care worker who is attempting to modify the organisational structure of their work place.

Arguably, the assertive approach to living is the clearest one when it comes to dealing with other human beings. The submissive person often loses friends because they came to be seen as duplicitous, sycophantic or as a 'doormat'. On the other hand, the aggressive person is rarely popular perhaps, simply, because most of us don't particularly like aggression.

The assertive person comes to be seen as an 'adult' person who is able to treat other people reasonably and without recourse to either childish or loutish behaviour. It has been suggested that the following are reasons why people should become more assertive:

- To cope effectively with unreasonable demands from others.

- To be able to make requests of other people.
- To ensure that personal rights are not quashed.
- To be able to withstand unreasonable requests from others.
- To allow for recognition of the personal rights of others.

All these functions can enable people to reduce their stress levels in interpersonal communication. Much has been written about the topic of assertiveness and the reader is referred to the recommended reading list at the end of this volume.

There are also certain behaviours that go with being assertive. A short list of these would include:

Eye Contact
The assertive person is able to maintain eye contact with another person to an appropriate degree.

Body Posture
The degree of assertiveness that we use is illustrated through our posture, the way in which we stand in relation to another person and the degree to which we face the other person squarely and equally.

Distance
There seems to be a relationship between the distance we put between ourselves and another person and the degree of comfort and equality we feel with that person. If we feel overpowered by the other person's presence, we will tend to stand further away from them than we would do if we felt equal to them. Proximity in relation to others is culturally dependent but, in a common-sense way, we can soon establish the degree to which we, as individuals, tend to stand away from others or feel comfortable near to them.

Gestures
Appropriate use of hand and arm gestures can add emphasis, openness and warmth to a message and can thus emphasise the assertive approach. Lack of appropriate hand and arm gestures can suggest lack of self-confidence and lack of spontaneity.

Facial Expression/Tone of Voice
It is important that the assertive person is congruent in their use of facial expression. Congruence is said to occur when what a person says is accompanied by an appropriate tone of voice and by appropriate facial expressions. The person who is incongruent may be perceived as unassertive. An example of this is the person who says he is angry but smiles as he says it: the result is a mixed and confusing communication.

Fluency

A person is likely to be perceived as assertive if he is fluent and smooth in his use of his voice. This may mean that those who frequently punctuate their conversation with 'ums' and 'ers' are perceived as less than assertive.

Timing

The assertive person is likely to be able to pay attention to his 'end' of a conversation. He will not excessively interrupt the other person, nor will he be prone to leaving long silences between utterances.

Listening

The assertive person is likely to be a good listener. The person who listens effectively not only has more confidence in his ability to maintain a conversation but also illustrates his interest in the other person. Being assertive should not be confused with being self-centred.

Content

Finally, it is important that what is said is appropriate to the social and cultural situation in which the conversation is taking place. Any English person who has been to the USA will know about the unnerving silence that is likely to descend on a conversation if he uses words such as 'fag' or 'lavatory' in certain settings! So will the person who uses slang or swear words in inappropriate situations. It is important, in being perceived as assertive, that a person learns to use appropriate words and phrases.

A paradox emerges out of all these dimensions of assertive behaviour. The assertive person also has to be genuine in his presentation of self. Now if that person is too busy noticing his behaviour and verbal performance, he is likely to feel distinctly self-conscious and contrived. It would seem that assertiveness training, like other forms of interpersonal skills training tends to go through three stages and an understanding of those stages can help to resolve that paradox:

- **Stage one** — the person is unaware of their behaviour and unaware of the possible changes that they may bring about to become more assertive.
- **Stage two** — the person begins to appreciate the various aspects of assertive behaviour, practices them and temporarily becomes clumsy and self-conscious in their use.
- **Stage three** — the person incorporates the new behaviours into their personal repertoire of behaviours and 'forgets' them but is perceived as more assertive. The new behaviours have become a 'natural' part of the person.

It is suggested that if behaviour change in interpersonal skills training is to become relatively permanent, the person must learn to live through the rather painful second stage of the above model. Once through it, the new skills become more effective as they are incorporated into that person's everyday presentation of self.

Becoming Assertive

In developing assertiveness in others, the trainer is clearly going to have to be able to role-model assertive behaviour herself. The starting point in this field, then, is personal development, if it is required. This can be gained through attendance, initially, at an assertiveness training course and later through undertaking a 'training the trainers' course. An increasing number of colleges and extra mural departments of universities offer such courses and they are often included in the list of topics offered as evening courses.

Once the trainer has developed some competence in being assertive, the following stages need to be followed in the organisation of a successful training course for others:

● **Stage one** — a theory input that explains the nature of assertive behaviour, including its differentiation from submissive and aggressive behaviour.

● **Stage two** — a discussion of the participants' own assessment of their assertive skills or lack of them. This assessment phase may be enhanced by volunteers role-playing typical situations in which they find it difficult to be assertive.

● **Stage three** — examples of assertive behaviour from which the participants may role-model. These may be offered in the form of short video film presentations, demonstrations by the facilitator with another facilitator, demonstrations by the facilitator with a participant in the workshop or through demonstrations offered by skilled people invited into the workshop to demonstrate assertive behaviour. The last option is perhaps the least attractive as too good a performance can often lead to group participants feeling deskilled. It is easy for the less confident person to feel 'I could never do that'. For this reason, too, it is important that the facilitator running the workshop does not present herself as being too assertive but allows some 'faults' to appear. A certain amount of lack of skill in the facilitator can be reassuring to course participants.

● **Stage four** — selection by participants of situations that they would like to practice in order to become more confident in being assertive. Commonly requested situations, here, may include:

— responding assertively to a colleague

— dealing with clients more assertively

— returning faulty goods to shops or returning unsatisfactory food in a restaurant

— not responding aggressively in a discussion

— being able to speak in front of a group of people or deliver a short paper.

These situations can then be rehearsed using the slow role-play method described above. At each stage of the role-play the participants are encouraged to reflect on their performances and adopt assertive behaviour if they have slipped into being either aggressive or submissive. Sometimes, this means replaying the role play several times. Another learning aid, here, is the use of what may be called 'perverse role-play'. Here, the various situations being played out are played out by the participants as badly as possible. In other words, the supposedly assertive person is anything but assertive and the 'client' behaves as badly as possible. It is often out of these perverse situations that new learning about what could be done occurs.

● **Stage five** — carrying the newly learned skills back into the 'real world'. Sometimes the very act of having practised being assertive is enough to encourage the person to practice being assertive away from the workshop. More frequently, however, there needs to be a follow-up day or a series of follow-up days in which progress, or lack of it, is discussed and further reinforcement of effective behaviour is offered.

Communication Skills Check List

● Assertiveness should be distinguished from aggressiveness.

● Consider the degree to which you are generally assertive, aggressive or submissive.

● Assertiveness takes practice: work at it.

● Try to attend an assertiveness workshop.

Activities for Skills Development

ACTIVITY ONE

In this section you are invited to decide to what degree you are assertive in your relationships with others. First, consider the following areas and think about the degree to which you deal assertively (or otherwise) with other people:

● at home
● at work, with colleagues, clients or patients
● with friends
● in shops.

ACTIVITY TWO

Now consider the following questions:

● Which style of confrontation describes your style best:
 — pussyfooting?
 — sledgehammer?
 — confronting?
● What (if anything) stops you from being assertive?
 — fear of rejection?
 — feelings of inadequacy?
 — feelings that other people are more important than you?
 — fear of reprisal?
 — other feelings?
● What do you need to do to become more assertive?
● What is likely to happen if you become more assertive?

This last question is an important one. If you are going to become more assertive, it is likely that other people will perceive you differently for a while. If you have had a tendency to be the 'pussyfooting' type, they are likely to see you as rather more pushy. If you have tended towards the 'sledgehammer' approach, they may see you as rather more subdued. Either way, other people are likely to be rather upset by your new 'presentation of self' and to want the 'old you' back. It is during this period that you need most courage and perseverance. The temptation to slip back to old ways is likely to be strong. If you want to deal with the world more on your own terms and to reduce the stress of always being subservient to the needs of others, such courage and perseverance pay off in the longer term.

ACTIVITY THREE

Observe your colleagues at work. Would you say that they are fairly assertive?

Communications Skills Questionnaire: Being assertive

Read through the items in the following questionnaire and tick the response that corresponds to how you feel about the statement. If you are working in a group, you may want to compare your responses to the statements. There are no right or wrong answers but the statements can help you to clarify your own thinking and beliefs about the topic.

1. I am not particularly assertive.

Strongly agree	Agree	Don't know	Disagree	Strongly disagree

2. It is not particularly important for me to be assertive.

Strongly agree	Agree	Don't know	Disagree	Strongly disagree

3. You get more assertive as you get older.

Strongly agree	Agree	Don't know	Disagree	Strongly disagree

4. Being assertive means being able to get angry with other people.

Strongly agree	Agree	Don't know	Disagree	Strongly disagree

5. You can't learn to be assertive.

Strongly agree	Agree	Don't know	Disagree	Strongly disagree

6. I would like to be more assertive.

Strongly agree	Agree	Don't know	Disagree	Strongly disagree

7. I get angry with other people fairly easily.

Strongly agree	Agree	Don't know	Disagree	Strongly disagree

8. I would say that I am a submissive sort of person.

Strongly agree	Agree	Don't know	Disagree	Strongly disagree

9. Men are generally more assertive than women.

Strongly agree	Agree	Don't know	Disagree	Strongly disagree

10. I intend to work on my assertiveness.

Strongly agree	Agree	Don't know	Disagree	Strongly disagree

Further Reading

Alberti, R.E. and Emmons, M.L. 1982 *Your Perfect Right: A Guide to Assertive Living*. Impact, San Luis Obispo, California.

Hargie, O., Saunders, C. and Dickson, D. 1987 *Social Skills in Interpersonal Communications*, 2nd edn. Croom Helm, London.

Heron, J. 1986 *Six Category Intervention Analysis*, 2nd edn. Human Potential Research Project, University of Surrey, Guildford.

Woodcock, M. and Francis, D. 1983 *The Unblocked Manager: A Practical Guide for Self-Development*. Gower, Aldershot.

8
Writing Skills

Keywords

- writing
- references
- publication.

We all have to write. Many of us will be asked to write reports of various sorts. Many will also be required to prepare essays and projects as part of course work on college courses. Some people find writing difficult, but the task is easier if basic rules of structure are adhered to. This chapter explores various aspects of writing, the overall aim is to make writing not only easier but enjoyable too.

Basic Principles

Although support workers face a variety of writing tasks, many of the rules of good writing apply to all. In this chapter we explore some of the principles of effective written communication.

First, the accent is on identifying certain basic rules. Then the focus shifts to keeping references. Any health worker who has to undertake basic or further education will be required to reference projects and essays. It pays to think a little about how such references may be recorded. In the later parts of this chapter, the discussion moves on to the layout of a written piece and then onto report writing and writing for publication.

What basic principles can be applied to all writing? A short list of such principles would include at least the following:

- Write short sentences.
- Write short paragraphs: three or four sentences is nearly always enough.
- Write to communicate, not to impress. Inflated language and extensive use of jargon rarely impress the reader, nor do they usually impress editors and managers.
- Avoid lengthy quotations of other people's work. Wherever possible paraphrase the writing of others, giving full acknowledgement to the original writer in the form of a reference, e.g. (Brown 1989).
- Write like you speak. Read through what you write and ask yourself: 'Would I say this?' If you wouldn't, think about how you could rewrite what you have written to make it more readable. People often make the mistake of thinking that 'correct' writing somehow sounds more intelligent than 'readable' writing.

Keeping References

Most support workers will be involved in courses. This usually means that they will have to write essays. This, in turn, means quoting references or indicating the books or papers that you have read. The important thing is to develop a system of recording that suits you best and that you will keep going.

Many people start a reference collection with good intentions only to discover that the whole thing becomes too cumbersome. As a general rule, keep the simplest records that you can but ones that will lead you straight back to the book or paper in question. The minimum that you will need to record for each item is:

- name of the author
- year of publication
- title of the book or paper
- publisher (if it is a book) or the name of the journal (if it is a paper).

Many people collect their references in a simple card file. Such files are readily available at stationers, as are the cards that go with them. Also available are index cards to keep them in order. It is usually better to choose the 8″ × 5″ cards, which allow for more detail to be recorded. A useful layout for a bibliographic reference card is shown in Figure 8.1. This card is then completed and

Author(s):	Year of Publication
Title:	
Publisher or name and details of journal:	
Location:	
Comments: Keywords:	

Figure 8.1 Layout for bibliographical reference card.

filed alphabetically under author. By using a comments section it is possible to record keywords for cross-referencing the item with other items and to save important quotes. A completed card is shown in Figure 8.2.

Andrews, P.	1990
Stress in Communication: The Health Worker's Dilemma	
Davis and Jones, London	
Location: Cardiff Central Library	
Comments: This has a useful review of theories of stress. Takes a 'biological' view of stress rather than a psychological one. 'Talk of stress is endemic in the health professions. It is as though the concept was quite new and necessarily dangerous' (p 16). Keywords: Stress, psychology, life sciences.	

Figure 8.2 Complete biographical reference card.

Card files are not the only way of recording references. Some people prefer to keep them in an index book. This is rather like a home telephone directory with index pages sticking out of the side. As new references are found, they are written into the appropriate section, alphabetically by author.

The other way of keeping references is to open a database on a computer. The advantage of this method is that as the list of references becomes larger, the computer database allows you instant access to particular items or sets of items. For example, you may want to find all of your references under the heading of 'psychology'. Whilst you could work through each of your cards and pull out all the appropriate ones, the computer database can do it for you almost instantaneously. It can also help you to prepare reference lists at the end of essays and projects.

Layout

Any writing that you do needs to be organised. The time to think about such organisation is before you start the writing. One of the most effective means of planning any writing project is through the use of *outlining*. These are the stages:

- **Stage one** — brainstorming. In this stage you write down, at random, any thoughts, ideas and hunches that you have about the writing project. Nothing is banned at this stage. The aim is to produce as many ideas as you can. Many will not be used in the project itself but, at this stage, the more varied, and even bizarre, the better. The odder ideas can lead on to more practical ones. Once you have filled a page with jottings of ideas in this way, you identify the ones that you will keep and strike out the others. Then, you look for 'patterns' in the ideas that remain and group them together. Finally, you move on to the next stage, the stage of beginning to organise your ideas more formally.
- **Stage two** — identifying key headings. Having identified some groups of ideas, the next task is to find headings for these groups. These headings then serve as the sections of your project. It is helpful to aim at between five and ten headings, whatever the nature of the project. If you are writing an essay, the ten can be ten themes that you address. If you are writing a book, the ten can be ten chapters.
- **Stage three** — identifying subheadings. Next, you carefully work through the list of headings and fill in the subheadings and possibly, the sub-subheadings. It is rarely useful to break up your work into more than three sets of headings. Once you have completed this stage, all that remains is to allocate a word limit to each heading and subheading and then to write out the body of the text.

The whole process of outlining in this way is speeded up with the use of a wordprocessing package on a computer. Then, the headings and subheadings can be moved around at will and new headings and subheadings added as necessary. There are outlining programs specially written for this purpose. An excellent one that is released as shareware (see page 106) is called PC Outline (see page 111). It allows you to generate as many ideas as you wish and then to organise them into a range of hierarchies, at will. Alternatively, you may find the whole process more easily carried out with an A4 pad and a pen.

Writing for Journals

Have you ever thought of writing for a magazine or journal? Most of us, once we have been in a health profession for some time, have built up a valuable store of information and opinion. It is important that everyone is prepared to share that with others. One means of doing this is through writing in a magazine.

Many health care workers write for journals and magazines. Many more do not. A number of people think that they could never get anything they wrote accepted for publication. On the other hand, others feel that an essay they have written for a course might make a good published article. It might, but there are better ways of doing things.

Writing for journals and magazines involves ensuring that you are very familiar with the publication you are writing for. So the first stage in getting into print is selecting the right journal.

There are two approaches to the second stage. Some people feel that it is best to write a letter to the editor outlining the proposed article. Others feel it is best to send off the manuscript and to let the editor decide on its strengths and weaknesses. I think the second way works better. The letter approach takes up more time and you may be asked to write a paper that was quite different to the one you had in mind. On the other hand, if you choose to send the manuscript off, directly, then you must make sure that it *exactly* fits the requirements of that journal. All health care journals publish 'instructions to authors' — usually at the back of each copy. Follow these to the letter. If you slip up on any one of the requirements, many journals will simply return your manuscript. Therefore, if the instructions ask for two manuscript copies, double line-spaced, on one side of A4 paper, send just that. Also send a covering letter stating that what you are sending is original and is not being offered to any other journal.

Never send duplicate copies of a manuscript to a variety of journals. What will you do if it is accepted by two? Also, some journals do not send out proofs for checking by the author. In this case, you would stand to risk the same paper being published in two journals. Attractive as this may sound, it is a sure way of encouraging editors never to take your work again.

When you send a manuscript off to a referred journal, it will be sent 'blind' to one or more professional referees. The 'blind', here, refers to the fact that your name will not be on the manuscript when the referees receive it. That way, they cannot be prejudiced by knowing your name.

After the referees or editors have made a decision, you may be asked to rewrite part of the paper. If you are asked to do this, do it exactly in the way that has been suggested. The reviewers and the editor, in this case, know best. Also, make the alterations as quickly and as accurately as you can.

Alternatively, your manuscript may be accepted outright. With acceptance, may come a letter offering you a fee on publication of the article. You can haggle over this figure but it is best to accept it in the early stages of your writing career. If you have submitted your work to a referred journal, it is unlikely that you will be paid for your work but the addition of a published article in a referred journal is usually a welcome addition to your CV.

Writing With A Computer

The next chapter discusses the uses of computers in various health-care-related projects. Here, the aim is to identify some of the ways in which using a computer can make a direct difference to the writing of projects, reports and articles.

Whilst not everyone gets used to writing directly with a keyboard, the fact that a paper or a letter does not have to be rewritten is the overriding advantage of learning to use a computer to communicate your thoughts. If you *do* decide to invest in and use a computer with a wordprocessing package, consider the following methods of making the process even easier:

- Work with the line setting set to single spacing, even though your final printout will be double-spaced. If you work with single line spacing, you can see more of your work and the eye does not have to move as far to scan the words. Scrolling through documents will be faster, too.
- Consider working with very wide margins whilst you are typing. This has the effect of making the screen look like this:

> The advantage of this sort of setting is that it allows you to see a lot of your work very easily. You no longer have to scan long sentences but, instead, your work is broken up into small, visible chunks.

- Try to learn *all* the functions of your wordprocessor. It is surprising how easy life can be once you let the computer do some of the more routine tasks for you.

- If your wordprocessor supports them, make liberal use of macros (the linking of a series of keystrokes to a single set of keystrokes). Well thought-out macros can save you time when cutting and pasting, spellchecking, wordcounting and backing up your work.
- Count words regularly. Regular word counts improve the style and consistency of your work by ensuring that you stick to the word limits that you set yourself at the proposal stage.
- Put references in at a later date if recalling them whilst writing is difficult. Simply place the code *** into your writing wherever a reference should appear, then, when you have finished the bulk of your writing, have the wordprocessor search for all the ***s and insert the appropriate references as you go.
- If your wordprocessor supports them, make good use of style sheets to ensure a uniform look to written work — particularly when you are writing a longer project, such as a thesis or book. Style sheets can ensure that all your chapter headings and subheadings are identical in style.
- If you have to print out a very long document on a dot matrix printer, consider printing it in bold and draft quality. This is much quicker than printing in near letter quality, and looks almost as good.
- Keep long documents divided into smaller sections by having a separate file for each section. Some wordprocessors allow you to pull a number of files together so that you can view the entire project as a whole.
- Consider laying out all your headings and subheadings for the entire project before you start to type the body of the text. This will ensure uniformity of layout and you will also be encouraged by the regular appearance of subheadings. This method also aids consistency and helps you avoid repetition.
- Despite all these suggestions, keep your wordprocessing simple. Avoid using fancy fonts and italics. If you want to indicate italics in a manuscript for publication, stick to using the underlining function.
- For work that is to be published, avoid elaborate diagrams, particularly ones that use vertical lines. Whilst your wordprocessor may be able to reproduce them, such diagrams are expensive to reproduce in published work.
- Write fast and edit later. One of the main advantages of wordprocessing is the editing facility. This relieves you from having to think too hard about spelling and sentence construction in your initial drafts.
- Back up your work as a matter of course. Do not be tempted to trust your hard disc, if you have one. All hard discs can fail at some time. If your wordprocessor allows it, set it to do automatic backups, while you work. Remember, though, that these backups are lost when you turn off the computer. If you are working on a large and important project, consider having at least two sets of backup discs. Keep them in

two separate places: one set at home and the other at work. Remember, though, to continue to back up both sets.

● Consider using a 'notepad' program (such as Sidekick), while you work in your wordprocessor. This allows you to make quick memos to yourself as you type. Otherwise, don't be afraid to leave yourself comments as you go. Again, use the *** symbol to indicate the beginning and end of such memos and later do a search for these symbols. The two sets will tell you where the 'memo' starts and ends.

● Consider running off a copy of larger projects in 'draft' printout mode. You can then use this to read through the entire project and you are free to scribble notes and changes all over it. A manuscript often 'reads' quite differently once it is printed out.

● Do not use headers or footers in your final manuscript. If these identify your name in a paper that is being sent out for 'blind' referring, then the editor will have to erase that name on each sheet. If you are submitting a book manuscript, the headers and footers will also have to be erased by a subeditor. Make sure, though, that you number every page.

● If you are using a dot matrix printer for printing out a thesis or book manuscript, make sure that you have at least two spare ribbons. I once tried printing out a manuscript on Sunday, with one, used ribbon — by page 300 the manuscript was unreadable.

Communication Skills Check List

● Writing is an important aspect of communication.

● There are some simple rules of writing that can make your writing more effective.

● It is possible to get your writing work published. Sharing your views about your work can add to the body of knowledge.

Activities for Skills Development

ACTIVITY ONE

Get a variety of books out of the library and read a few pages of each book for the *style* of writing. What could you say about the style of writing in *this* book?

ACTIVITY TWO

Start to keep a list of the books and articles that you read. Keep a set of cards as described in this chapter.

ACTIVITY THREE

Write out a plan for an article for a magazine that you read. Begin with broad headlines and then fill in the subheadings. If you can, go ahead and write the article.

Using the Skills: Spotting the Problems

Read through the following passage. Using the skills described in this chapter, try to identify where the piece falls down as an attempt to communicate. How would you edit the passage?

Explanatory report about an incident in the Jeffrey James Unit

I was on the late shift at the unit and I had been delegated the responsibility of attempting to ensure that all of the residents were adequately cared for and I was doing this to the best of my ability. Mr Sharp, the person in charge of the Unit left the Unit for a few moments and I was left alone because he had gone out. When I went into the day room I found that Mrs Irene Andrews had fallen on the floor and was lying down in an awkward position and did not seem to be moving although she seemed to be breathing and I thought that she was probably not seriously ill or unwell. I ran forward to check that she was breathing and found that she was. I made no attempt to move her feeling that it was better to leave her as she was. I asked her if she was alright and she said that her leg hurt. Shortly afterwards, Mr Sharp returned to the unit from his visit away from the unit and I reported what I had found to him. He undertook responsibility for ensuring that the doctor was called as a matter of urgency and the matter was resolved in this way. I am in the employment of the Unit as a care assistant and my tasks involve a variety of caring roles which I attempt to carry out as part of my duties. I have been in the employment of this Unit for about 16 months and have not had an incident of this sort occur before and I would hope not to have one again although I would say that it was not possible to predict the fall of Mrs Andrews. I think that I did what I could to look after her after her incident had occurred and I made sure that she was not moved once she had fallen as this could have caused more injuries including some internal ones.

Communications Skills Questionnaire: writing skills

Read through the items in the following questionnaire and tick the response that corresponds to how you feel about the statement. If you are working in a group, you may want to compare your responses to the statements. There are no right or wrong answers but the statements can help you to clarify your own thinking and beliefs about the topic.

1. My writing style is generally good.

Strongly agree	Agree	Don't know	Disagree	Strongly disagree

2. I keep a note of all of the books and articles that I read.

Strongly agree	Agree	Don't know	Disagree	Strongly disagree

3. 'Style' in writing is not so important as content.

Strongly agree	Agree	Don't know	Disagree	Strongly disagree

4. I am not sure there is much I can do to improve my writing.

Strongly agree	Agree	Don't know	Disagree	Strongly disagree

5. Many people in the health care fields do not write very clearly.

Strongly agree	Agree	Don't know	Disagree	Strongly disagree

6. Clear writing is an important part of communicating with others.

Strongly agree	Agree	Don't know	Disagree	Strongly disagree

7. I intend to work at improving my writing.

Strongly agree	Agree	Don't know	Disagree	Strongly disagree

8. I intend to try to write a short article for publication.

Strongly agree	Agree	Don't know	Disagree	Strongly disagree

9. I would like to write using a computer and will try to in the near future.

Strongly agree	Agree	Don't know	Disagree	Strongly disagree

10. I can think of three writers that I would like to be able to imitate for their style.

Strongly agree	Agree	Don't know	Disagree	Strongly disagree

Further Reading

Turk, C. and Kirkman, J. 1989 *Effective Writing: Improving Scientific, Technical and Business Communication*, 2nd edn. Spon, London.
Wells, G. 1981 *The Successful Author's Handbook*. Macmillan, London.

9
Computing Skills

No one in the health care field can go very far without encountering computers in one form or another. The present generation of children and students is growing up completely computer-literate. Older health care workers may be struggling to come to terms with using computers. Either way, many people arrive at the point where they have to decide whether to buy one.

If they *do* decide to buy one, they have next to think about what sort and about what software to buy. In this chapter, we explore aspects of buying and working with home computers and computers at work. Many of the issues in this chapter will also apply to working with computers in both clinical and community settings.

Buying a Computer

Why buy a computer at all? Many people are finding that they are useful for a range of applications in the home (Burnard 1989). The usual reason for buying one, as far as health care workers are concerned, is for completing course work towards further education or degree studies, or for research work.

Other obvious applications in the health care field and home context are:

- for keeping notes
- for maintaining bibliographies and book lists
- for doing accounts
- for keeping address and contact lists.

What computer should you buy? Computer hardware (the keyboard, monitor and computing unit itself) is changing rapidly. It is also dropping in price. Any specific advice about particular models of computer would be out of place. Certain general suggestions may be made. A computer for use in the home, that is not going to age too quickly should fulfil most and perhaps all of the following criteria:

- It should be IBM compatible. IBM set a certain standard for computing equipment at the end of the 1980s. Whilst many computers are 'IBM clones', and whilst it is not necessary to buy a genuine IBM machine, it is essential that the computer that you buy is fully compatible with IBM machines.
- It should have a hard disc. A hard (as opposed to a floppy) disc is capable of storing vast amounts of data. Whilst larger capacity floppy discs are being developed, hard discs currently allow for the storage of 20, 40, 70, 100, 300 megabytes (Mb) of data and above. The hard disc also allows you to store all your programs inside the computer and saves you having to find discs and load up programs from 'outside'.
- It should be expandable. Many computers have 'expansion slots' inside them, which allow for upgrading in line with current technological developments. Some of the cheaper and smaller ones do not. It is not necessary to keep changing hardware to keep up with every development. On the other hand, if you do not keep up with some of the *main* developments, you may find that you can no longer find software to work with your computer as it gets older.
- It should have a monitor and keyboard that suit you. On the monitor issue, many feel that a black and white screen is ideal for wordprocessing. On the other hand, some feel that a colour screen gives them more flexibility. Others prefer a large size screen that allows them to see and work on a whole A4 page of print at a time. Obviously, larger screens also

cost more and are 'non-standard'. Similarly, the 'feel' of a keyboard is the subject of much debate. Some prefer a keyboard that reminds them of a typewriter and 'clicks' when the keys are pressed. Others prefer a 'deader' keyboard. It is recommended that you try typing on a range of keyboards before you choose yours. This is one of the problems when buying computers through the post. Unless you have had experience of the model that you order, you will not be able to try out the keyboard before you buy.

● It should have sufficient RAM (random access memory) to allow you to use modern programs. As computers develop, so the random access memory requirements grow. Until fairly recently, a computer that had 640 kilobytes (k) of memory was thought to be adequate. Then the usual figure was 1Mb. Now it is not uncommon to find machines with 4–8Mb fitted as standard. If you cannot afford to buy a computer with a lot of RAM fitted as standard, make sure that you can expand the memory at a later date.

Where should you buy a computer? It is sometimes tempting to walk into high street branches of electrical stores and wander round their computer departments trying to decide what you should buy. This is fine if you know what you are looking for but the assistants in such shops are rarely computer experts. It is probably better to enlist the help of a computer expert at work — someone who knows about your own work and your own computing needs. Most health organisations have one or two resident computer bores — you shouldn't have to look far.

You should also become familiar with the computers that you have at work. Learn about them, their capacities and their costs. Then get to know the computer magazines and begin to compare prices. Often, the process of buying through the post can be an excellent way of getting a good computer at a fair price. The obvious limitation is that you must know what sort of computer you want. Also, make sure that the firm that you buy it from offers you after sales service.

Whilst most computers are fairly reliable and have relatively few moving parts to break down, it is important that you can get help on the spot when you need it. Watch out for the companies that insist on a 'back to base' warranty. This means that if your computer breaks down at home, you are responsible for returning it to the company.

There is never a 'right time' to buy a computer. It seems to be a fact of life that just as you get your first computer, you come to realise that it is already out of date. This is just a reflection of the rapid development of the computing industry that shows no sign of levelling off. You just have to live with it.

Once you have bought your computer (or better still, before you buy it) learn to type. It is surprising how many people still use the 'hunt and peck' approach to the keyboard and continue to type with two fingers. Part of developing keyboard skills is learning to type. Two approaches are possible here:

- Attend an evening class in typing, or find an intensive weekend workshop.
- Buy one of the many software packages that allow you to develop typing skills at the keyboard. Such programs offer a graded and timed approach to learning how to type and are a cost-effective and time-economical way of advancing keyboard skills.

Using a Computer

Get into the habit of working in a consistent way with your computer. If you have a hard disc, make sure that you organise your files on it in a logical way. With the large amounts of space available on such a disc, it is quite easy to lose files if you do not organise them into directories and subdirectories. The manuals that come with your computer when you buy it will tell you how to do this.

The one golden rule of computing is to make frequent backups of your work. That is to say that you always have more than one copy of every file that you work on. Then, if a file gets lost, destroyed or 'corrupted' in some way, your work has not been lost.

This rule is particularly important if you have a hard disc. It is easy to adopt the habit of believing that hard discs are reliable and not subject to breakdown. Generally, this is true. The point is, though, that hard discs have a finite life. At some point, they all *do* break down. If this happens and you have not made backups of your work, your work is lost. Make backups of all the writing that you do and of any new data files that you work on. If, for example, you add references to your bibliographic database (see page 87) make sure that you back up the database onto another disc.

Wordprocessing

The wordprocessor is probably the most frequently used program in any home or office computer. What can it do? Essentially, it allows you to edit and re-edit your work without having to retype everything that you have written. Compare this with typewriting. If you use a typewriter and make a mistake, you have two options:

- you use a correction paper or fluid and risk making a mess of the page
- you retype the whole page.

With a wordprocessor, neither of these options is necessary. If you make a mistake, or if you want to reorder paragraphs or change the text completely, you merely go back up the screen and make the changes. Only when you are completely happy with what you have written do you print out your final 'hard' copy. Wordprocessors vary immensely in their complexity. As with all things, you tend to get what you pay for: the more fully featured programs tend to be very expensive.

Check before you buy a wordprocessor that (i) you need all the features on offer, and (ii) you will be able to learn how to use it fairly easily. Like other skills, wordprocessing takes practice. It is not like sitting down at a typewriter and beginning to type. You need to invest some time in learning how to use a wordprocessing program. Such learning is repaid by cleaner pages, better organised work and the knowledge that you are no longer frightened of computers. Some of the important features to look for in a wordprocessor are:

- the ability to move text easily
- a spellchecking routine
- a feature for wordcounting
- the ability to work with more than one document at once
- the ability to insert page numbers.

As you become more proficient at wordprocessing you may want to move up to a more comprehensive program, especially if you do a lot of business, academic or creative writing. Other, more advanced features include:

- an indexing facility
- the ability to work with graphics, diagrams and boxes
- a thesaurus facility
- a function for pulling together a number of files
- macros, or the ability to enter a string of commands with a single key stroke.

Spreadsheets

A spreadsheet program allows you to develop a huge 'rows and columns' chart on your computer. It does more than this: it also allows you to undertake a whole range of calculations on each, or on a selection, of the rows and columns. In some ways it is like a computerised and automated accounts book. On the other hand, it can also do far more than just compute rows and columns. It can be used for at least the following functions:

● storing addresses
● compiling bibliographies and reference lists
● drawing 'word illustrations' in column format.

Graphics

Graphics packages allow you to illustrate and generally 'dress up' your work. A top commercial package will help you to do the following:

● generate graphs, histograms and pie charts
● use 'clip art' to illustrate news letters and projects (Clip art is a selection of copyright-free illustrations available on disc)
● make slide presentations
● generate charts for use as overhead projections in teaching
● draw organisation charts.

A good graphics program can help to make your work look more professional and can help you to communicate your thoughts through iconic representation. A basic rule applies here, though: keep it simple. Graphics programs can generate very complicated illustrations and diagrams. It is easy to get carried away with what they can do. Communication is generally much clearer if you stick to simple charts and representations.

Databases

After the wordprocessor, the database program is probably one of the most useful for the student, teacher and practitioner in the health care field. Essentially, a database program helps you to store information in a readily retrievable format.

The obvious use of a database in this context is for storing references and bibliographies. Databases can also be used for storing other sorts of information from simple names and address lists through to patient records. Clearly, if the latter are being kept, it is important to see that you comply with the Data Protection Act. Database programs will usually allow you to:

● index your information in various ways
● print reports of selected information
● transfer information from the database to other programs
● allow 'mailmerging' or the generation of multiple letters addressed to different people.

Again, the keyword is simplicity. Commercial database programs are very powerful and often quite difficult to learn to use. If your aim is to keep track of a number of bibliographies, try one of the simpler database programs. Alternatively, you may decide merely to keep your bibliographies as files within your wordprocessor. There are a number of advantages to this approach.

First, you can very readily transfer information from the data file to the one you are working in; second, you do not have to close down one program in order to access your lists of references; third, you do not have to learn another program. On the other hand, a database program will be much faster and much more versatile if you have bibliographies that run into the hundreds of references. I used a file in my wordprocessor to list all my references until the number reached about 500. Then I switched to using a database for them and found the increase in speed and accessibility paid off considerably.

Some people never use databases for storing references and prefer to stick to a card file. The argument is usually that it is just as quick to flip through a box of cards for a reference as it is to start up the computer and fire up the database program. This is fine if the card file is not too big.

The point about a database program is that it can let you make 'selective' searches of your references and can allow you to print out those selective searches. For example, it can let you pull out all the references that you have on counselling or all those by a particular author *and* about a specific topic. It can show you all of the papers written on a particular topic after or before a certain date and so on.

Another sort of database that can be particularly useful is the 'free-form' database. Most programs ask you to decide, beforehand, on the format of the information you will enter into your database. For example, you may be required to decide on whether or not you include, in a bibliographic database, all or none of the following: author, date, title, publisher, place of publication. You are also asked to decide, beforehand, how *much* data you will enter into each section. The free-form database does away with this restriction. With this sort of program, you merely enter any notes or details that you want, in any format. The program then allows you to find that data on another occasion, as long as you can remember one of the words in the data. Free-form databases allow you to work very flexibly with notes of varying lengths, references, appointments and so forth.

I use a free-form database called Memory Mate, in which I store all my book and article references (at the moment about 1000) and all sorts of names, addresses and notes. I can recall any item in one or two seconds. Consider using a free-form database if you know that your requirements for storing information are going to be varied.

Commercial Software

Commercial software refers to the programs that are sold on the open market and produced by software companies. Many of the best-known programs are very expensive to buy. On the other hand, they are nearly always very reliable and trustworthy. They also come with very detailed handbooks about their use. If you buy commercial software, only you are allowed to use it. You cannot make copies of it for your colleagues and friends.

The example of a book is a useful one here. If you buy a book, you can *lend* it to another person and whilst they have it, you cannot read it. What you must not do is to photocopy that book. Commercial software usually works on a similar principle. Once you have brought a copy of a program, it must only be used by one person at a time and copies must not be made for distribution to others.

The only exception to this general rule is that most companies allow you to make a 'backup' copy of the program in case the original discs get damaged. Figure 9.1 offers examples of some commercial programs.

Commercial Wordprocessing Programs
WordPerfect
WordStar
Word
Commercial Spreadsheet Programs
Lotus 1–2–3
Quattro
VisiCalc
Commercial Database Programs
dBASE
Paradox
FoxPro

Figure 9.1 Examples of commercial software programs.

Shareware

Shareware has a unique marketing strategy. A shareware program is distributed free of charge (although a charge is usually made for the discs and the handling). The idea is that you first try the program and then, if you like it, you send away a registration fee to use it.

In the first instance, you usually have between 30 and 90 days to try out the program before you register it. Further, during this time, you are encouraged to make copies of the program for your colleagues and friends. Then, the same principles apply: they are allowed to try out the program and then send off to become registered users if they find it useful.

The advantages of the shareware approach are many for the home PC user. First, he or she gets a chance to try the program before making a financial commitment to it. Second, the registration fees for shareware are considerably cheaper than the cost of copies of most commercial programs. Also, the quality of shareware programs is improving all the time and some of the best is easily the equal of commercial software.

Finally, shareware offers you an easy approach to learning more about computer programs and to exploring a variety of methods of working with data that you may not have been able to try if you had to rely on buying commercial packages. The names and addresses of shareware distributors are available in any of the monthly computer magazines. Such magazines often include one or two shareware programs on a 'free' disc attached to the front cover.

Shareware is not free. The idea, as we noted above, is to try out the program, decide if you like it and then pay for it. If you decide not to use the program then you simply give the discs to another person or format the discs for use with other files. The only free programs are those available in the *public domain,* ie copyright-free. These public domain programs are often distributed by the same people that handle shareware although it is often not made clear in their catalogues what is shareware and what is public domain.

A wide range of shareware is now available and, in the paragraphs, below, some of the more well known ones are briefly described to help you with what sometimes seems to be a bewildering choice.

Wordprocessors

Galaxy Lite
This is a very simple but very usable wordprocessor that operates with simple pulldown menus. It can do all the usual things a wordprocessor can do, including moving blocks of text, deleting text, searching and replacing and so on. It also has a spell checker but, for some reason, does not have a word counter.

On registration, you receive the latest version of the program, a full instruction manual and detailed spell checker. The program works in RAM and takes up very little disc space. It is therefore a particularly useful program to use with a small laptop or notebook computer where disc space is limited. Also, because it works in RAM, it does not often access the disc and thus it saves battery power.

New York Word

This is a very powerful wordprocessing package that will be very useful if you need to use a lot of wordprocessing functions. New York Word allows you to customise the program to suit your own needs and preferences.

Mindreader

This is an unusual wordprocessing program. Whilst, at one level, it works in much the same way as many others – via menus – it also has an unusual function in that it anticipates the word that you are typing and, as required, types out the rest of the word, before you do. Thus, if you use the word 'bibliography' very frequently, it will offer to type out that word once you have typed in the first two letters. This is a particularly useful program if you tend to be a rather slow typist. On the other hand, the program's anticipations of your words can, of course, be wrong and this can slow you down.

PC-Write Lite

This is another popular and easy-to-use wordprocessor that comes complete with a spell checker and word counting function. Included with the program is a tutorial that allows you to get to grips with all of the functions of this major program.

Sage Words

This used to be sold as a commercial wordprocessing package. It is easy to learn and to use and covers all the functions that you would expect to find in a wordprocessor. The layout of this program is rather similar to that of the commercial package, WordStar. If you are familiar with that program you should have no difficulty in getting to grips with this one.

Spreadsheets

As Easy As

This is named with reference to the best selling commercial spreadsheet program, 1-2-3 produced by Lotus. It is said by many to be as good if not better than many commercially sold spreadsheet programs. It is easy to set up and run and you can transfer data in and out of the program to and from other programs.

Quebecalc

This is an unusual program in the shareware catalogue in that it allows you to work with more than one spreadsheet at a time and allows you to develop three-dimensional spreadsheets. This is particularly useful if you need to compare and contrast numerical data.

Turbo Calc

This is another powerful and easy-to-use program. It supports many mathematical, statistical and financial functions and comes with full documentation.

Databases

PC-File

Again very powerful and easy to use, PC-File can be used 'intuitively' by simply following the instructions on the screen, although full documentation comes with the discs. PC-File allows you to develop large or small databases and is ideal for keeping bibliographic reference listings or details of club membership, names and addresses and all the other things that people normally use a database program for.

File Express

Another easy-to-use database program that does not have quite the same number of functions as PC-File but which is very easy to set up. Again, this program is very useful for keeping a list of the books that you read and wish to refer to again. If you are on a training course and have to write essays and projects, a program like this is very useful for collecting the bibliographic information.

Zephyr

This is a very powerful program that is easily comparable to many commercial programs costing hundreds of pounds. However, you will have to learn how to use it, as it is not so 'intuitive' in its use as the previous two programs.

Menu Systems

Some people find the 'command line' of MS-DOS or other operating systems difficult to work with. Menu systems allow you to link up your programs to a menu that appears on screen every time you turn on your computer. Old hands at computing tend to think this is a form of cheating but most of us are happy with anything that makes life easier.

Still River Shell

This comprehensive menuing system allows you to start up programs, check and move files and has many other useful features to make your computing life easier.

Treetop

This allows you to do all of the file management tasks that you need and also allows you direct access to your programs without going through the operating system.

Stupendos

This is a very popular, easy-to-use menu system that offers a wide range of functions. Stupendos makes working with files on a hard disc particularly easy.

Other Useful Shareware Programs

The Ultimate Diary

This is a computerised organiser. It allows you to work with a programable diary and record all your appointments for as long as you need. You can also use it as a journal and for recording personal and work-related issues.

Ticklex

This is another organiser that offers an alarm system to remind you of appointments (or anything else) on a particular day, when you turn on your computer. It also has a diary and a to-do list feature.

Instant Recall

This is a very useful, free-form database. Most database systems require that you decide, before you start using the program, the format of the information you will be entering. Thus, if you are recording book references, you have to decide that you will first enter the author's name, then the date, then the title and so on. With a free-form database, there are no such restrictions (see page 104). You merely type in whatever it is you want to record and can then search the whole record out again later. I have found this flexible program very useful for recording the details of books and other references and have also used it in the analysis of research data. It is worth making sure that you register this program as the full version is much more powerful.

Easydraw

This is a general purpose drawing program that allows you to draw lines, circles, squares and so forth with considerable precision. It also allows you to develop flowcharts.

ZipKit

This series of programs allows you to compress your files so that they take up less disc space. This approach to disc management is particularly useful if you work with floppy discs and want to keep down the number of discs that you use. It is also helpful if you use a hard disc and want to make economic use of it.

PC-Draft

This graphics program allows quick and easy picture-drawing on the screen. It comes complete with a 30-page instruction manual on disc. As usual with this sort of program, you can draw squares, lines, circles and insert text into diagrams and pictures.

Kwikstat

For those who need to use statistical calculations, this is a complete set of short programs that allow the quick computation of a range of statistical tests. It is menu-driven and easy to use as long as you know the sorts of statistical calculations you need to do. As always with statistical packages, it is important to know the appropriate tests to use with the data you have.

Flashback

If you use a hard disc, it is vital that you backup everything that is on it onto floppy discs. It is not a question of *if* your hard disc fails you will lose all your data, it is a question of *when* your hard disc fails. Like all mechanical systems, the hard disc will one day stop working. Flashback is a simple-to-use program that helps you to back up your work to floppies.

PC-Tutor

This is useful if you are new to computers. It is an on-disc tutorial that introduces you to all aspects of computing from making subdirectories to copying discs. This is an easy way of getting to know how to get the best out of your computer.

4DOS

This program offers you an extension of the operating systems MS-DOS and DR DOS. Simple to use, 4DOS offers more than either of these systems, and is also user-friendly.

PC-Iris

If you need to undertake confidential work and it is important that you can lock your files, this is the program to do the job. It allows you to attach a codename to your files in such a way that anyone without the codename will not be able to open them.

Letters and Labels

With this program you can set up an address list of up to 1800 names and addresses. The program also helps you to print out labels using some or all of these addresses. This is particularly useful if you have to contact all of your clients through a mailing circular.

PC-Outline

This is a famous program and a classic one. It enables you to work out the structure of essays, projects or 'to do' lists by helping you to develop a series of headings and subheadings. You can, at any time, rearrange your list of headings, delete them or add new ones. Whilst you can do all this with a pen and pad of paper, PC-Outline tends to save you a lot of time and seems to encourage creativity.

Cliché Finder

If you tend to write badly or suspect that your writing is a little 'tired', this program will examine your file and pull out all the clichés. There are several shareware programs of this sort; this is just an example of one of them.

Sharespell

This is a straightforward spell checking program for use if your wordprocessor doesn't have one.

PC-Deskteam

This is a collection of programs, including a clock (which can chime if necessary), a text editor, a calculator, a notepad and various other 'desktop' features. This can be run as a 'terminate and stay resident' program, which means that it can be made to 'pop up' over any other program that you are working with and then 'popped down' again. This would be useful, for example, if you wanted to leave your wordprocessor, briefly, to add up some figures. When you have done your calculation, you can return to exactly the same spot in your wordprocessor file. Again, there is a variety of programs of this sort available as shareware and many of them are very easy to use and very useful.

PC-Graph

The name of this program tells you what sort of program it is. It allows you to enter data and to plot a graph from them. The graphs can then be stored for reproduction at a later date.

This is a small selection of some of the many programs that are available as shareware. Remember that shareware programs are *not* free programs. Once you have decided to continue to use a program, you are trusted to register the program with the author or the publishing company. It is worth noting, though, that shareware registration prices are always considerably lower than the cost of commercial packages and the programs are often just as good.

An example of such a program is PC-File, which is widely used in place of commercial packages because it is so easy to use and yet very powerful and fast.

Various other sorts of programs are useful to the health care worker. Some of them are commercial programs but a good many are available as shareware. A short list of these other types of software would include:

● statistical packages
● personal organisers and diaries
● accounting packages
● computer-aided drawing programs
● desktop publishing programs
● educational programs
● aids to learning about computing
● programs that allow you to communicate with other computers.

Modems

As your knowledge and use of computers increases, and as computing equipment becomes cheaper, you may want to consider buying a modem. A modem allows you to send computer files down a standard telephone line to another computer. It also allows you to contact other computer users through 'bulletin boards' or computerised message stations. A considerable amount of shareware is available through this means, as is some public domain, or free, software.

A modem can also aid communication between where you work and where you live. You may choose, for example, to work at home on certain days and to send in your work via the modem. This is of particular value to those who engage in writing reports and printed matter.

Communication Skills Check List

● Make yourself familiar with the computers that are used where you work – ask if you can see what they are used for.

● Consider taking a short course in computer skills.

● Remember that you do not have to be able to program to use a computer.

● Consider whether or not a computer would help you with your own studying and working.

Activities for Skills Development

ACTIVITY ONE

If you have not used a computer before, find a friend or a colleague who has one and ask him or show you what it can do. Ask them to go slowly as they show you the computer. It is easy to feel 'blinded by science' in the early days of becoming computer literate.

ACTIVITY TWO

Buy a copy of a computer magazine. Work through the advertisements and note down the different sorts of hardware (the machinery part of the computer) and the different types of software (the programs that the computers run). Work out what sort of computer would best suit your needs and decide on any software that you would need.

ACTIVITY THREE

Find out what computers and software are used in the organisation in which you work. If you can, try to get access to the computer and learn to use it.

Communications Skills Questionnaire: Computing skills

Read through the items in the following questionnaire and tick the response that corresonds to how you feel about the statement. If you are working in a group, you may want to compare your responses to the statements. There are no right or wrong answers but the statements can help you to clarify your own thinking and beliefs about the topic.

1. I'm not sure that it is necessary to know how to use computers to work in the health care field.

Strongly agree	Agree	Don't know	Disagree	Strongly disagree

2. I don't think I will ever understand computers.

Strongly agree	Agree	Don't know	Disagree	Strongly disagree

3. It is important for me to increase my knowledge of computers and to learn to use more software.

Strongly agree	Agree	Don't know	Disagree	Strongly disagree

4. It is not necessary to know anything about programming to use a computer.

Strongly agree	Agree	Don't know	Disagree	Strongly disagree

5. Most health care workers use computers at some stage of their work.

Strongly agree	Agree	Don't know	Disagree	Strongly disagree

6. I am determined to learn more about computers.

Strongly agree	Agree	Don't know	Disagree	Strongly disagree

7. Computers can take over some of the more mundane clerical tasks and free up time to spend with clients.

Strongly agree	Agree	Don't know	Disagree	Strongly disagree

8. Some people are naturally good at using computers.

Strongly agree	Agree	Don't know	Disagree	Strongly disagree

9. I will eventually buy a computer.

Strongly agree	Agree	Don't know	Disagree	Strongly disagree

10. Most people I know well are computer literate and able to use computers fairly easily.

Strongly agree	Agree	Don't know	Disagree	Strongly disagree

Further Reading

Burnard, P. 1990 So You Think You Need a Computer? *The Professional Nurse,* **6(2)**, 119–20.
Ball, M.J. and Hannah, K.J. 1984 *Using Computers in Nursing.* Reston Publishing, Reston, Virginia.

10
Telephone Skills

Keywords

- telephone skills
- answering
- telephone manner
- telephone counselling.

We all use the telephone but who uses it well? This chapter explores some aspects of making effective use of the telephone. As a means of communication, it has limitations. You cannot see the person you are talking to, therefore it is impossible to 'read' the non-verbal communication of the other person. This is also an advantage. Some people find face-to-face communication difficult when they are actually with another person. This is particularly true when emotional topics are being discussed. Sometimes, the anonymity of the telephone makes it a really therapeutic instrument: hence the success and value of the Samaritans organisation. With the Samaritans, total confidentiality is offered. The person calling in does not see the person who is helping and vice versa. The fact that the Samaritan service works so well suggests that this mode of communication is often a useful one.

Many people are nervous of the telephone. Some actively avoid using it if they can. Yet a considerable amount of work in the health services is done on the telephone. Consider, for example, the following settings, which all rely on the use of the phone:

- offering emergency counselling
- ensuring that elderly people have a 'life line'
- keeping contact with clients in rural areas
- working in the evenings with clients.

Without the phone, these services would be greatly diminished. Telephone skills, then, are an essential part of learning to communicate.

What are Telephone Skills?

Telephone skills include, at least, the following:

- making a call
- answering the telephone
- taking accurate messages
- telephone counselling.

If you find that you *are* nervous of using the telephone, try the following form of 'flooding'. For the next few days, try to do as many things as you can via the telephone. Phone up to see whether or not particular shops are open. Ring the leisure centre before you go swimming to check opening times. Ring local papers and ask for the advertising rates. Answer the phone as frequently as possible. During all of these activities, notice the following aspects of the call:

- what you say
- your tone of voice
- whether or not you smile when you talk on the phone
- how you are greeted by others
- their tone of voice
- what you say when you pick up the phone.

These aspects of using the phone are crucial to becoming skilful in this domain. First, think about what you say when you pick up the phone. Perhaps the least useful thing you can say is simply 'Hello'! When answering the phone, it is useful to say the following three things:

- a greeting
- where you are speaking from (i.e. your place of work, etc)
- your name.

It is reasonable, then, to consider saying something like: 'Hello. This is the Aden Road Health Centre, Carl Jones speaking.' If you usually just say 'Hello', you will find this quite a mouthful. Try ringing various companies, however, and you will generally find that this is the format that they use. The method not only conveys just the right information to the caller but it helps to set a welcoming tone to the conversation; it also saves time. The caller does not have to ask various questions to establish that he or she is through to the right organisation and the right person.

As you speak, smile. Obviously the other person cannot see you but a smile can be detected in the voice. If you find this hard to believe, practice recording your voice onto a tape recorder: smiling and not smiling. See if you can tell the difference. Sometimes, it is quite dramatic.

When you answer the phone, keep a pad of paper and a pen with you all the time. As the person says their name, jot it down on the pad. Then, later in the conversation, you can use their name when saying goodbye ('Goodbye, Mrs Jones and thank you for calling'). This method not only shows that you are interested in the caller but it again saves time. You never have to ask the caller their name a second time.

It is also a good idea to note the time of the call. This is particularly important if it is likely that the call is for someone else. As you take down the message, you can record, with accuracy, the time the call was taken. To this end, too, it is useful to invest in some of those pads which read 'While you were out . . . called.' Such pads tend to offer you a check list of important information to take down. If you do not use such a pad, make sure that you take down the following information:

- the name of the caller
- the time the call was taken
- whether or not the other person is to call back
- the name of the person to call back
- the telephone number of the person to call
- the suggested time of the return call
- any message that goes with the call.

If the call is for you and it does not involve telephone counselling, keep it short. Remember that telephone calls are expensive and also that other callers might be trying to get through. Become expert at summarising what the other person is saying and make sure that you have their full name and telephone number if any action is to be taken. Again, if the call is for you, it is still useful to jot down the name of the caller and the time of the call. This is a useful way of 'logging' the use of the phone and of noting who calls in to your department.

Avoid giving people what the Americans call the 'runaround'. That is to say, if you cannot answer a telephone query, find someone who can. Avoid vague and inaccurate statements such as:

'I'm not sure, but I think it might help if you contact the Town Hall. They tend to be able to deal with problems like yours. I think you'll find that they help . . .'

If you don't know the answer to something, say so. If you can't find someone in your department to help but know that there is someone who can, take down the caller's name and telephone number and promise them that the person will call back. Then, make sure the person in your department gets the message.

When you are talking on the phone, remember to speak clearly. It is surprising how many people mumble into the phone and this is probably an indication of nervousness. In ordinary conversation, we rely on non-verbal aspects of speech to help us decipher meaning. On the phone, we have no such indicators. If you are constantly being asked to repeat what you say, speak up a little. On the other hand, make sure that you don't shout down the phone. Most of us have had experience of people who sound as though they are shouting from the next room when they are on the phone.

Again, practice your telephone manner with a tape recorder. The easiest way to do this is to do it very privately — when everyone has gone out. Also, there is absolutely no need to tell other people what you are doing, so that you only embarrass yourself once — when you use the tape recorder! Bear in mind that most of us are shocked when we first hear ourselves on tape.

If you find that your voice is very monotonous, try exaggerating a highly modulated tone, just to see what the other extreme sounds like. You will probably be surprised by how unexaggerated it sounds when you play it back. Listen to announcers on the radio or television and notice how much they modulate their voices. This is particularly noticeable if you turn off the television picture and just listen to the spoken voice. Most people who work in television can use their voices very effectively. You can also learn to use yours effectively on the telephone.

Answerphones

Many people do not like speaking to answerphones. However, they are essential parts of the communication system in many businesses and many aspects of health care work. Don't ring off. Wait until you hear the bleeps and then take a deep breath and speak slowly and clearly.

Keep your message short and take particular care with saying your telephone number slowly and distinctly. If it is a long number, use 'chunking' when you give the number. That is to say, divide the number into three digit 'runs' ('223 . . . 345 . . . 464). Don't just run the whole number off in one, long breath.

I use an answerphone machine to take calls when I am out of my office. I often have to replay calls two or three times to make out the phone number of the person who has called. Because *we* are familiar with the number, we often don't think to slow down our delivery for the other person.

Also, spell out unusual names — and particularly names that are in another language. For example, I live in a street called 'Y Dolydd' — a Welsh name. If you are Welsh, you will know that it is pronounced very differently to how it is spelt. If in doubt, spell the words onto the answerphone. The same can be said about your surname if it is in any way unusual. You are familiar with it but other people will not be.

If you have to prepare an answerphone message, there are some basic principles to bear in mind. Do not, for instance, say that 'I am sorry but I am out at the moment . . .' If you live in an area where the burglary rate is high, this is an open invitation. Instead, suggest that you are 'unable to take your call at the moment . . .' Keep your message short and remind the caller to speak clearly after the tone. A suitable message is:

'Hello, this is David Jones. I am not able to take your call at the moment but if you leave your name and number, I will get back to you as soon as I can. Please speak clearly after the long tone.'

Again, the tape recorder can be useful, here, for trial runs. Many people adopt a rather strange voice when first recording messages on an answerphone. A few trial runs can help to make the message bearable. Remember that your message can help the person to decide whether or not they will call back or whether they will ring off. You want them to do the former.

Telephone Counselling

Sometimes, people ring because they are desperate. If this happens, it helps if there is someone to hand who you can hand over to. Unfortunately, it occasionally happens that there is no one else around and you are called upon to do some very basic telephone counselling.

It is not being suggested that by reading this section you will in any way be able to describe yourself as a counsellor but it is important to identify some ways of helping another person who needs emergency help. The important issues in working through a crisis with someone who phones are:

● Concentrate on helping the person to stay on the phone. Be encouraging in your manner and, if necessary, ask them for a phone number where you can phone them back.
● Listen, listen again and then listen some more.
● Concentrate on helping them to talk about their feelings rather than on detailed problem-solving; the problem-solving can come later.
● If they know you well, ask them if they can come to your place of work or, if it is appropriate, arrange for them to be visited.

● Report the conversation to someone else as soon as possible and make sure that a senior person is fully aware of the nature of the call.

Detailed telephone counselling is a skilled job and is done particularly well by some of the telephone counselling agencies that exist for a range of problems. If you can, visit a telephone counselling service and ask them about their training and about how they do their work.

Pay particular attention to the way that telephone counsellors answer the phone, keep the other person talking and the way that they *listen*. The anonymity of the telephone is one of its great advantages in some forms of counselling. The fact that when you talk to a counsellor on the phone they cannot see you and you do not have to give your name, can free you up to talk more easily about your problems.

Not everyone finds it easy to talk in this way on the phone, and not everyone finds it easy to help other people on the telephone. Either way, though, as a health care worker, you need to be as effective as you can in working with the telephone. Judging by the reception it is possible to get when phoning large hospitals, there is still a lot of work to be done in this area.

Get into the habit of listening to how people answer the phone when you ring a variety of organisations and businesses. Note the ones that have clearly given some thought to the way that they present themselves in public. Notice, too, the ones that seem less interested in acting as ambassadors in this way. Think, carefully, about what it is that makes for a successful 'telephone manner' and decide whether or not *you* have to do anything to improve yours.

Communication Skills Check List

● It is important to become skilled in using the telephone.

● Keep a pad by the phone so that you can record the name of the person who is calling and the time at which they called.

● Practice using the telephone as much as possible if you are nervous of using it.

Activities for Skills Development

ACTIVITY ONE

This week, notice how you answer the telephone when you are at work. Just observe, at this stage and do not try to change your style.

ACTIVITY TWO

Think of ways that you could be more effective on the phone. Write out a plan of action and then implement the plan.

ACTIVITY THREE

Listen to colleagues using the phone and observe their *behaviour* as they talk. Also notice whether or not they appear to be good listeners.

Using the Skills: Spotting the Problems

Read through the following telephone conversation. Using the skills described in this chapter, try to identify as many mistakes in communication as possible and identify ways in which those mistakes could be rectified or could have been avoided.

'Hello'
'Hello, is that the Health Centre?'
'Yes'
'Is Mrs Davies there?'
'No, not today.'
'When will she be in?'
'I'm not sure.'
'Will she be in tomorrow?'
'I think so, probably.'
'Who is that speaking?'
'David'
'David?'
'David Green.'
'Oh, hello David.'
'Hello.'
'Could I leave Mrs Davies a message, please?'
'Yes. I'll just get some paper.'
  . . .
  . . .
'I'm sorry, I can't find any paper but I'll tell Mrs Davies when I see her.'
'Could you tell her that my Digoxin tablets have run out and that my 5 mg Valium tablets are the wrong strength . . . she'll know what I mean.'
'OK then.'

'Will you tell her for me?'
'Yes.'
'Goodbye, David.'
'Goodbye.'

Communications Skills Questionnaire: Telephone skills

Read through the items in the following questionnaire and tick the response that corresponds to how you feel about the statement. If you are working in a group, you may want to compare your responses to the statements. There are no right or wrong answers but the statements can help you to clarify your own thinking and beliefs about the topic.

1. Most people use the phone well.

Strongly agree	Agree	Don't know	Disagree	Strongly disagree

2. There is no need for specific training in using the phone.

Strongly agree	Agree	Don't know	Disagree	Strongly disagree

3. I don't mind talking to answerphone machines.

Strongly agree	Agree	Don't know	Disagree	Strongly disagree

4. I could do a lot to improve my telephone skills.

Strongly agree	Agree	Don't know	Disagree	Strongly disagree

5. Most health care workers do not use the phone very well.

Strongly agree	Agree	Don't know	Disagree	Strongly disagree

6. Telephone skills offer a method of developing therepeutic conversations.

Strongly agree	Agree	Don't know	Disagree	Strongly disagree

7. Most clients are nervous of the phone.

Strongly agree	Agree	Don't know	Disagree	Strongly disagree

8. It is impossible to talk openly on the phone.

Strongly agree	Agree	Don't know	Disagree	Strongly disagree

9. I tend to mimic the person at the other end of the phone, when I am talking to someone.

Strongly agree	Agree	Don't know	Disagree	Strongly disagree

10. More training in telephone skills should be offered to all health care workers.

Strongly agree	Agree	Don't know	Disagree	Strongly disagree

Further Reading

Burnard, P. 1988 Communicating on the telephone. *Senior Nurse*, **8(13)**, 14 – 18.
Dillman, D.A. 1978 *Mail and Telephone Surveys*. Wiley, New York.

11
Self-awareness

Keywords

● self-awareness
● reflection
● relaxation
● feelings.

We all need to be self-aware. If we are to offer effective care to others we must first get to know ourselves better. This chapter explores the concept of self-awareness as it applies to working as a health care worker. It also offers practical activities for enhancing your own self-awareness.

What is Self-awareness?

Self-awareness is the process of getting to know your feelings, attitudes and values. It is also learning about the effect you have on others. We can never say that we have become self-aware. We are always in the process of getting to know ourselves better. Consider the following situations:

● You are talking to a patient who has been bereaved recently. She starts to cry. As she continues to talk and cry, you find yourself on the verge of tears. Why?

- In a children's ward, a child starts shouting. You find yourself increasingly irritated and then annoyed by the shouting. Why?
- A colleague is rather sharp with you. You find yourself very hurt by what she says and unable to throw off the comment. Why?

There are no single or straightforward answers to any of these questions. Developing self-awareness can help you to find *your* answers to them. The fact that we all lead different lives, have different histories and are pleased or upset by different things means that we all react to situations differently. The process of becoming self-aware is a personal journey of discovery. It is a process which can help you to be more effective as a health care assistant.

Why Become More Self-aware?

This could all be a bit self-indulgent. Why should anyone spend time on getting to know themselves better? Life is difficult enough without spending hours worrying about who you are or about the meaning of life. These are some people's reactions to the idea of self-awareness. The question remains, though: why should health care workers develop self-awareness? Consider the following situations:

- A client begins to shout abuse at David, a health care assistant. At first, David takes this personally and is upset by it. Slowly, though, he realises that the abuse is part of that patient's way of coping with his illness. David appreciates that the man's anger is not directed against David but against his own illness.
- Debbie works in an adolescent unit. She avoids Katy, a young girl who is suffering from anorexia nervosa. Debbie tells her colleagues that she has no sympathy with Katy and feels that she has nothing to say to her. As the days go by Debbie realises that one of the reasons that she avoids the girl is because Katy reminds her of herself. This realisation helps Debbie to strike up a helpful relationship with the other girl.
- Andy thinks that he is far too quiet in group discussions in the unit. He feels inadequate and thinks that everyone else is both brighter and quicker than he is. On reflection, though, he comes to appreciate that he is *different* to some of the other nurses and health care assistants. He begins to appreciate that not everyone has to be chatty or talkative and that lots of people like him *because* he is quiet.

These are some examples of how self-awareness can help in caring for and working with other people. The fact that we understand ourselves a bit more can make life easier: both for other people and for ourselves. Specifically, self-awareness can help in the following ways – it can:

- Help us to appreciate the difference between us and other people.
- Enable us to acknowledge that we are different.
- Help us to realise that other people are different too.
- Enable us to see that not everyone thinks and feels in the same ways.

How do you Become Self-aware?

As we have seen, self-awareness is a *process*. We never arrive at the goal of self-awareness, we are always travelling towards it. As we grow (how ever old we are) we continue to change and develop; we never stand still. Becoming self-aware is a lifelong process. In this section, we identify some basic methods of self-awareness development. In the section that follows are some activities for encouraging you to reflect on who you are and what you think and feel.

Reflection
This is the most straightforward method of all. All you have to do is to *remember to notice yourself*. This sounds so simple that it can sound silly. But stop for a moment and notice yourself now. For example:

- What are you thinking about?
- What are you feeling at the moment?
- What does your body feel like?
- How tensed or relaxed are your muscles?

Answering these questions can lead to a small increase in self-awareness. It is surprising how often we turn ourselves on to automatic pilot and fail to notice what we are doing, thinking or feeling.

This is the starting point: remembering to reflect. It can become a way of life. Next time you find yourself upset by something a patient says to you, stop and notice what is happening to you. What are you thinking? What are you feeling? What is your body doing? These three domains can form a simple self-awareness checklist. Try to remember to notice, as frequently as possible:

- your thoughts
- your feelings
- your body.

Keeping a Diary
This is reflecting through writing. Many people start a diary at some time and let it drop after a few days or weeks. Yet a diary is a useful way of developing self-awareness. One way to overcome the problem of keeping it up is to *structure* the diary. One of the things that causes people to stop writing is they come

to the conclusion that they 'don't have anything to write'. This is where the structure can help. Some headings that can be useful are:

- reflections on present thoughts and feelings
- reflections on work
- new skills learned
- books or articles read
- relationships.

You may want to add or subtract headings from this list. The point is to rule up a series of pages in a book with these headings and to use them to help you to clarify your thoughts and feelings.

Some people find it helpful to discuss what they write in their diaries with other people. Other people feel that they are completely private documents that they wouldn't show to anyone. If you are of the latter view, think about what may happen if other people *did* read your diary. What would they learn about you from it? What do you feel you have to hide from others? What would happen if you told other people about these aspects of you?

One of the interesting things that have come out of psychotherapy is that what we see as most personal about ourselves are often the things that almost everyone sees as most personal. It is as though we are all going around desperately trying to keep secrets about ourselves and yet those 'secrets' turn out to be true of nearly everyone! If you *do* share what is in your diary with a small group of other people, notice the degree to which this is true. Notice how other people's 'skeletons in the cupboard' are often your own. Underneath, it seems, we are probably all alike.

Relaxation

Learning to relax can help in the process of becoming self-aware. The connection may not be obvious at first. Think about it: if you are constantly tense and nervous, you are not experiencing life to the full — you are too preoccupied. Also, tension and anxiety can help us to take a negative view of ourselves. We don't see the positive aspects of ourself, only the negative. Relaxation can help us enjoy ourselves more and thus get to know ourselves a bit better. Stop for a moment and check how relaxed or tense you are at the moment.

The giveaway signs of tension are usually found in the muscle clusters. Check how relaxed or tense the muscles in your neck and shoulders are. How well are you concentrating on reading this book? Is concentration easy or do you find yourself distracted by all sorts of thoughts that come flooding into your head? If you *are* tense, what is the tension about: what is causing it? All these questions can help in the process of getting to know yourself better. Once you have identified whether you are tense, you can decide whether or not you want to do anything about it!

A simple way of experiencing relaxation is through the use of a relaxation exercise. If you can, try the one that follows. Find a quiet place where you will not be disturbed for about half an hour and read through the following script to yourself. As you become familiar with the script you will find that you 'know' it and no longer need to read it. Consider using it regularly if you are prone to tension. Once you have used it to relax, lay back and appreciate the difference between being tense and relaxed.

Lie on your back, with your hands by your sides . . . stretch your legs out and have your feet about a foot apart . . . Pay attention to your breathing . . . take two or three really deep breaths . . . now allow your head to sink into the floor . . . your head is sinking into the floor and you begin to feel more and more relaxed . . . allow your brow to become smooth and relaxed . . . feel your cheeks relaxing . . . let your jaw drop and relax . . . feel the tension draining out of your temples as your jaw relaxes . . . let yourself relax . . . more and more . . . let your shoulders drop and feel your neck and shoulders relax . . . more and more relaxed . . . now become aware of your right arm . . . let your right arm become heavy and warm and relaxed . . . your upper right arm . . . lower arm . . . your right hand . . . the whole of your right arm is heavy and warm and relaxed . . . no tension . . . just relaxed . . . now become aware of your left arm . . . let your left arm become heavy and warm and relaxed . . . your upper left arm . . . lower arm . . . your left hand feels heavy and warm and relaxed . . . the whole of your left arm is heavy and warm and relaxed . . . your shoulders and chest feel relaxed . . . your abdomen feels relaxed . . . your pelvis and hips . . . you're feeling heavy and warm and relaxed . . . your right leg and foot feels heavy and relaxed . . . your left leg feels the same . . . your whole body is relaxed . . . no tension . . . just relaxed . . . and you can appreciate what it feels like to feel safe and warm and relaxed . . . just lay back and enjoy the feeling . . .

Now, slowly, stretch yourself . . . stretch your arms and legs . . . your toes and fingers . . . now slowly sit up . . . taking your time . . . slowly sit up and take a few deep breaths . . . and appreciate what it feels like to feel really relaxed.

Expressing Feelings

Many people bottle-up their feelings. Often it seems easier to do this than to risk embarrassing yourself by expressing them. Working in health care settings means coming into contact with a lot of people who are in varying degrees of emotional distress. In the past, it was considered 'professional' to learn to deal with people who were emotionally upset by remaining very much 'in control'. Health care workers were expected to hide their feelings. Yet they were never given any training on how to do this or on why it should be done.

Arguably, it is healthier to learn to express feelings rather than hide them. Not that you can always express feelings just when you feel them. If, for example, a patient is very upset, it might not help to get very upset yourself — at the time. Afterwards, however, it may be very useful to talk the episode over with a supportive friend and, if you want to, express your *own* feelings.

The business of learning to cope with feelings is two-fold. First, you have to learn to notice your own feelings. Then you have to learn to express them. If you are already a person who can express feelings fairly easily, such advice will seem odd. There are plenty of people, however, who have lost track of how they feel and almost never express feelings openly.

Here is a simple activity that you can use to identify some of your own feelings. Lie down somewhere quiet and allow yourself to relax. Then allow yourself to review your life *backwards*. Start with the present and gradually work back through the years, slowly reviewing your life events. Go back as far as you can go. As you do this, notice your changing moods and feelings. Notice, too, the parts of your life that you move over quickly. Notice whether or not you enjoy doing this activity.

The next stage is to allow yourself to talk through some of the more difficult parts of your life with a trusted friend. You have to choose the right time to do this. Clearly, not all of your friends will appreciate you suddenly telling them all about your past! Do it slowly and allow yourself to relive some of the feelings that you associate with particular times. Gradually, if you do this, you will feel yourself 'thawing out'.

As you thaw out in this way, make a pledge with yourself that you will no longer bottle things up quite so much. Become determined to share feelings with other people on a regular basis. This does not mean that you have to start crying easily or getting angry in all the wrong places. It just means that you agree to express feelings a little more regularly. As a result, you will probably find that you handle other people's emotions more easily. One of the problems with bottling up feelings is that we find other people's feelings difficult to cope with. Other problems associated with bottled-up feelings include:

- physical tension
- a feeling of emotional 'numbness'
- getting snappy for no apparent reason
- becoming 'moody'
- dealing with things on a 'theoretical' rather than an 'emotional' basis
- feeling cut-off from other people.

Overall, then, the benefits of learning to cope with and release feelings tend to outweigh any initial embarrassment you may feel about the prospect.

Communication Skills Check List

● Self-awareness is an essential part of being a helper in the health care field.

● We become more self-aware as we reflect on what we do.

● If we can acknowledge our feelings as we experience them, we are likely to get to know ourselves better.

● We cannot *always* be self-aware.

● Relaxation can help us to communicate with others.

In the sections above, we have discussed some of the ways of becoming self-aware. By far the most important one is learning to reflect and notice what you are thinking and feeling. The following activities build on the ones described above. You can either try some of them now, choose to do them later or decide to try them with a small group of colleagues or friends. Often, self-awareness development is more fun and more revealing when it is done in the company of other people. The key, though, is to keep the atmosphere in such a group fairly light and comfortable. Nothing inhibits a self-awareness group more than the atmosphere becoming too heavy and earnest.

Activities for Skills Development

ACTIVITY ONE

Without stopping to think about each one, read through and finish the following sentences. Once you have done this, go back and reflect on your answers. If you do this activity in a group, have each person finish one sentence, round the group, before moving on to the next.

The thing that interests me most is . . .
The sort of person I find most difficult is . . .
I would describe myself as . . .
The thing I dislike most is . . .
If I was famous I would . . .
The worst thing about me is . . .
The best thing about me is . . .
The sort of person I would like to be is . . .
I get angry when . . .
I am easily embarrassed by . . .
I don't like . . .
I appreciate . . .
When I was at school, I . . .
My parents are the sort of people who . . .
The job that would suit me best would be . . .
If I had lots of money I would . . .
When I get upset, I . . .
The things I like best are . . .
The place I would most like to live is . . .
The sort of person I find most difficult to work with is . . .

ACTIVITY TWO

Try observing the following 'ground rules' in conversation for the next few days. Alternatively, use these ground rules in a group discussion:

- Say 'I' rather than 'you', 'we', or 'people'. Thus, say 'I get angry when I hear things like that' rather than 'Things like that tend to make people angry'.
- Speak directly to other people rather than 'about' them. Thus, say 'You are irritating me' rather than 'Some people around here can be very irritating'.
- Take some risks in disclosing things about yourself to others. If you are naturally prone to keep yourself to yourself, try sharing something of yourself with others.

ACTIVITY THREE

Try paying conscious attention to everything that is going on around you for a period of ten minutes. If you are sitting reading this book, stop; put the book down and look around you. For ten minutes, take in everything that you can see, hear or smell. Also, pay close attention to any thoughts and feelings that crop up. Do not try to stop those thoughts or feelings but allow them to happen and accept them. Try this activity on a regular basis.

ACTIVITY FOUR

Continuing the Process
This chapter has discussed some of the reasons for developing self-awareness and has described some methods of becoming self-aware. Don't leave it here. Read some more about self-awareness and the ways that you can develop it. Most of all, practise some of the methods described here and see the difference they make to your everyday nursing practice.

Communications Skills Questionnaire: Self-awareness

Read through the items in the following questionnaire and tick the response that corresponds to how you feel about the statement. If you are working in a group, you may want to compare your responses to the statements. There are no right or wrong answers but the statements can help you to clarify your own thinking and beliefs about the topic.

1. I know myself fairly well.

Strongly agree	Agree	Don't know	Disagree	Strongly disagree

2. I need to develop more self-awareness.

Strongly agree	Agree	Don't know	Disagree	Strongly disagree

3. No one can teach another person to be self-aware.

Strongly agree	Agree	Don't know	Disagree	Strongly disagree

4. Most of my colleagues are already self-aware.

Strongly agree	Agree	Don't know	Disagree	Strongly disagree

5. Self-awareness is essential if we are to be therapeutic.

Strongly agree	Agree	Don't know	Disagree	Strongly disagree

6. Self-awareness can be an uncomfortable process.

Strongly agree	Agree	Don't know	Disagree	Strongly disagree

7. I would like to get to know myself better.

Strongly agree	Agree	Don't know	Disagree	Strongly disagree

8. If I knew myself more, I would tend to get less stressed.

Strongly agree	Agree	Don't know	Disagree	Strongly disagree

9. There should be a greater emphasis on self-awareness in health care training programmes.

Strongly agree	Agree	Don't know	Disagree	Strongly disagree

10. Self-awareness is important for clients as well as staff.

Strongly agree	Agree	Don't know	Disagree	Strongly disagree

Further Reading

Bond, M. 1986 *Stress and Self-Awareness: A Guide for Nurses*. Heinemann, London.

Burnard, P. 1990 *Learning Human Skills: An Experiential Guide for Nurses*, 2nd edn. Heinemann, Oxford.

Claxton, G. 1984 *Live and Learn: An Introduction to the Psychology of Growth and Change in Everyday Life*. Harper and Row, London.

Porritt, L. 1990 *Interaction Strategies: An Introduction for Health Professionals*, 2nd edn. Churchill Livingstone, Edinburgh.

12
Putting It All Together

Keywords

- self-management

- assessment

- curriculum vitae

- values clarifications.

Learning to communicate is a lifelong process — we begin it at birth and we probably never complete the whole of it. We learn as we go. This book has been about specific aspects of communication. It has offered skills and ideas for helping in the process of becoming a more effective communicator. It has noted, too, that communication in the health care field takes many forms: from one-to-one conversation with colleagues and clients, through group discussions and therapy to communicating in other forms — via computers and in writing.

It is suggested that to become a competent communicator in the 1990s it is important to be a good all-rounder. The person who really does communicate well, does so both verbally and through written media.

The aim of this last chapter is to pull the threads together and to offer some examples of how effective communication can make a difference to our work in the health care field.

Self-management

The first stage in managing your own communication skills is assessing them. In the following pages, you are asked to reflect on the skills described in this book and assess your own skill levels. There are no numbers to add up or results to work out but working through the questions can help you to find out what you need to do next.

If possible, work through these pages with a colleague or friend. It is helpful if you can talk about the various elements as you go. It is also useful if you can get someone else's opinion of your skill levels. We are not always the best judge of how we communicate with others: sometimes, other people can help us identify our strengths and deficits.

Each of the boxes, below, refers to a particular skill. Beneath each heading, you are asked to note which of the statements most nearly applies to you.

Listening and Attending	Tick a box
1. I am very good at listening to others and usually give them my full attention.	
2. I can listen fairly well but I am easily distracted.	
3. I find listening to people difficult and prefer talking.	
4. I am not very good at listening at all.	

Talking: Giving Information	Tick a box
1. I usually give appropriate and clear information.	
2. I give as much information as possible whenever I can.	
3. I like to assesss what information people want before I offer it.	
4. I don't particularly like giving information to people.	

Talking: Supporting	Tick a box
1. I am usually very supportive of other people.	
2. I can support people but have my limits.	
3. I prefer other people to be supportive.	
4. Trying to be supportive makes me anxious and I am not very good at it.	

Talking: Drawing Out	Tick a box
1. I can draw people out fairly easily and enjoy doing it.	
2. I can sometimes draw people out but I don't often achieve it.	
3. I find drawing people out difficult.	
4. I try to avoid drawing people out.	

Talking: Confronting	Tick a box
1. I can confront effectively when I need to.	
2. I tend to be more aggressive than confronting.	
3. I tend to be more submissive than confronting.	
4. I don't like confronting people at all.	

Talking: Coping with Emotions	Tick a box
1. I cope with other peoples' emotion well.	
2. I can cope if someone cries but I don't feel very comfortable.	
3. I would call someone to help if someone started to cry.	
4. I do not like coping with other peoples' emotions at all.	

Opening a Conversation	Tick a box
1. I can start conversations very easily.	
2. I can start a conversation with some difficulty.	
3. I try to let the other person start the conversation.	
4. I find the whole topic very difficult.	

Structuring a Conversation	Tick a box
1. I find it easy to control and structure a conversation.	
2. I do not normally think about structuring.	
3. I usually leave the structuring of a conversation to the other person.	
4. I prefer to be 'natural' in a conversation.	

Ending a Conversation	Tick a box
1. I can usually end a conversation quite easily.	
2. I often find it difficult to end conversations.	
3. I usually wait till the other person finishes the conversation.	
4. I find ending conversations very difficult.	

Working in Groups	Tick a box
1. I enjoy group work and find no difficulty in working with groups.	
2. I am sometimes unsure what to say in group meetings.	
3. I would rather not work in groups.	
4. I try to avoid groups.	

Running Groups	Tick a box
1. I would enjoy chairing or facilitating a group meeting.	
2. I think I could run a group if I was asked to.	
3. I would feel very uncomfortable if I was asked to run a group.	
4. I could not run a group.	

Being Assertive	Tick a box
1. I think I am assertive.	
2. I am more aggressive than assertive.	
3. I am more submissive than assertive.	
4. I am not sure whether or not I am assertive.	

Writing Skills	Tick a box
1. I write fairly clearly and well.	
2. I need to improve my writing skills.	
3. I do not write well.	
4. I try to avoid putting things in writing.	

Computing Skills	Tick a box
1. I am quite happy using computers of different sorts.	
2. I can use a computer but not very easily.	
3. I don't know much about computers.	
4. I avoid computers if possible.	

Self-Awareness	Tick a box
1. I think I know myself reasonably well.	
2. I need to get to know myself better.	
3. I am often surprised by the things that I do.	
4. I don't think I know myself at all.	

Once you have worked through these boxes, discuss your findings with your colleagues. See what they think of your answers. This process of getting feedback from others is a useful means of assessing ourselves. We no longer have to rely only on our own opinion of ourselves but we can compare that opinion with that of people who know and work with us.

If you are called upon to give another person feedback about his or her skills level, remember to be tactful. Offer your assessment 'cleanly'. That is to say, do not qualify it or wrap it up. For example, try not to use phrases such as: 'You are good at listening but I think you need to work harder at it.' This sort of feedback is confusing. If possible, avoid 'but' statements.

Keeping a Record

As you develop your life and communication skills, it is important to keep a record of what you have done. Increasingly, employers will ask you for your CV (curriculum vitae — literally 'life curriculum'). It helps to start keeping one early on in your working career and to keep it up to date as you change.

Curriculum Vitae

Before you work on your CV it is useful and interesting to map out your life to date. This can help you to remember your achievements and can also help to develop self-awareness. Further, it can be an aid to deciding what you want to do next in terms of your career or your personal life. Buy a notebook and write out a 'life-line' by starting from your earliest memories. The following headings will help you to recall some of the details of this personal biography.

● very early memories: preschool
● primary schooldays
● early friends and friendships
● early relationships with parents

- changing school
- secondary schooldays
- new friends
- adolescence
- changing relationships with parents
- first boy- or girl-friends
- sexual experiences
- social development
- physical changes
- early job aspirations
- examinations
- early work experience
- political views
- religious views
- leaving school
- college, university or further studies
- changing views
- travel
- any moves of house or district
- current work
- current relationships
- hopes for the future
- plans
- current beliefs and values.

As you work through this list of headings, note the degree to which you stay the same and the degree to which you change. Think about the way that your communication skills have changed or developed since your early schooldays. What influenced the way you communicate — your parents, teachers, friends?

Once you have carried out this research into your own biography, you can begin to compile your CV. You will find the biography will help you to put the various items into order. The following are the headings for information that you will normally put into your CV. The other point about keeping information in this way is that it can help you when you are asked to fill in an application form. It is often difficult to remember exact dates of schooling and examinations. The up-to-date CV means that you always have this information to hand.

Headings for a Curriculum Vitae

- full name
- address
- age

- nationality
- marital status
- educational record (dates of schools and colleges attended, starting with the most recent and working back)
- qualifications (record everything: GCSEs, A levels, certificates, diplomas, degrees, etc.)
- current job
- name and address of your current employer
- number of years and months in present post
- summary of responsibilities in current job
- previous work experience (include everything: work experience gained at school, YTS schemes, part-time weekend work, etc.)
- courses attended (through school, college or work)
- publications (if applicable)
- awards (swimming, Duke of Edinburgh's awards, etc.)
- interests away from work
- name and address of two referees (*always* ask before you put peoples' names in this section. Try to make sure that one of the referees is familiar with your recent work and that one is familiar with your school or academic work. Only ask people who you know will give you a *good* reference!)

If you have a computer, it is easiest to keep your CV as a file in your wordprocessing program, then you can frequently update it. When you come to print it out, spend some time in thinking about the format of the final print out. Keep it conservative, though. Nothing looks worse than a CV that has been produced with a Desktop Publishing Programme and looks as though it is nearly ready for publication as a local newspaper! Keep your CV business-like, clear and plain. Future employers are not likely to be impressed by a fancy layout but *will* be impressed by a thorough and well-thought-out CV.

Communication Reviewed

As we have noted throughout this book, it is really important to clarify personal values: what we believe and hold to be important. Appropriately, then, this book ends with a series of questions for you to consider about your own values, beliefs and attitudes towards all aspects of health care work and towards communication in particular. Work through them slowly, perhaps in pairs or in a group.

Consider what your answers to them are *now* and what your answers might have been a year or more ago. This will help in reviewing how far you have come and where you have come from. As for the rest: keep working at improving your communication skills. We all need help and we all need to improve. We are all, everyone of us, learning as we live. I hope this book has helped a little in the process of focusing on some of the issues involved in that complicated but intriguing process: communicating with other people.

Values Clarification: Questions About Personal Values

1. Do you think that people are responsible for themselves?
2. Do you think that we are also responsible for other people?
3. Should people be forced to take care of themselves whenever they can?
4. Can communication skills be taught?
5. Have they been taught to you?
6. Who do you know that communicates very well?
7. What do they *do*?
8. Do you like them?
9. What is it about people that you don't like?
10. Who is the person that you know that is most like you?
11. Who is the person that you know that is most different to you?
12. Of all the people that you know, who is the most important?
13. What are the things that you like most about people?
14. What are the things that you like least about people?
15. What do you like most about yourself?
16. What do you like least about yourself?
17. Do you believe in God?
18. Do you think that people *ought* to believe in God?
19. Do you think that you have changed very much over the past five years?
20. In what ways do you need to change more?
21. What is it about you that has stayed the same?
22. Are you responsible for everything that you do?
23. Do you think that people should talk freely about sex?
24. What *wouldn't* you talk about to other people?
25. Do you mind if people ask you what you earn?
26. Are you happy with your job or your course?
27. Do you think that you are intelligent?
28. Do you think that you are attractive?
29. Do you think that people do not know the 'real' you?
30. What sort of work would you do if you did not work with people?
31. Do you feel that most health care workers do their work effectively and therapeutically?
32. What political views do you hold?
33. Can you imagine changing those views?

34. Where did they come from?
35. What would you most like to change about the world?
36. Could you imagine being a conscientious objector?
37. Would you say that you were aware of 'green' issues?
38. Generally speaking, do you like other people?
39. Would you say that you were an optimist?
40. Are you happy with life?
41. Who are you most afraid of?
42. Who would you most like to get to know better?
43. What is the most difficult thing about working with other people?
44. Do you lose your temper easily?
45. What are your views on marriage?
46. Should gay people be allowed to 'marry'?
47. Do you think that abortion should be available on demand?
48. Are you fully aware of how AIDS is transmitted?
49. Are you a cautious person?
50. Are you a good communicator?
51. How would you react if you found out that you were HIV-positive?
52. What is the worst thing that could happen to you?
53. If you could travel anywhere in the world, where would you go?
54. Could you imagine being a monk or a nun?
55. What is the most difficult thing you have ever had to do?
56. Have you ever broken the law?
57. Do you think that the prison system is a good one?
58. If you were to change sex, what sort of man or woman would you be?
59. If you could live anywhere, where would you choose to live?
60. Do you think the world has changed very much in the last five years?
61. Do you consider yourself British or European?
62. Have you travelled widely?
63. Would you say that you were broad-minded?
64. How would you like to change your appearance?
65. What is the worst thing about you?
66. What is the best thing about you?
67. Do you have a sense of humour?
68. Do you watch 'soaps' on television?
69. Do you think that people watch too much television?
70. Are you careful about what you eat?

Communication Skills Check List

● Good communication is communication through *all* media — conversation and computers.

● The effective communicator is one who can choose the right medium for the right occasion.

● We are all, constantly, learning about communication.

● Communication is a lifelong process.

Activities for Skills Development

ACTIVITY ONE

Skip-read each chapter of this book and make notes about how *you* relate to each chapter. Note, too, the parts of the book that you disagree with.

ACTIVITY TWO

Start a journal of your progress in becoming a better communicator.

ACTIVITY THREE

From today, begin to observe other people as they communicate. Note, particularly, their *behaviour* and what they *say*.

Communications Skills Questionnaire: Communication in the health field

Read through the items in the following questionnaire and tick the response that corresponds to how you feel about the statement. If you are working in a group, you may want to compare your responses to the statements. There are no right or wrong answers but the statements can help you to clarify your own thinking and beliefs about the topic.

1. I need to pay more attention to the ways in which I communicate.

Strongly agree	Agree	Don't know	Disagree	Strongly disagree

2. I can think of other ways of communicating that are not described in this book.

Strongly agree	Agree	Don't know	Disagree	Strongly disagree

3. Communication is a central part of the health care process.

Strongly agree	Agree	Don't know	Disagree	Strongly disagree

4. We all communicate all of the time, whether we like it or not.

Strongly agree	Agree	Don't know	Disagree	Strongly disagree

5. Most of my colleagues communicate fairly effectively.

Strongly agree	Agree	Don't know	Disagree	Strongly disagree

6. I am determined to improve my communication skills.

Strongly agree	Agree	Don't know	Disagree	Strongly disagree

7. I will read more about communication theory.

Strongly agree	Agree	Don't know	Disagree	Strongly disagree

8. I will observe my behaviour when I communicate, in future.

Strongly agree	Agree	Don't know	Disagree	Strongly disagree

9. No one can teach you how to communicate effectively.

Strongly agree	Agree	Don't know	Disagree	Strongly disagree

10. You can't learn how to communicate out of a book. You have to do it.

Strongly agree	Agree	Don't know	Disagree	Strongly disagree

Further Reading

Claxton, G. 1984 *Live and Learn: An Introduction to the Psychology of Growth and Change in Everyday Life*. Harper and Row, London.
Simon, S., Howe, E. and Kirschenbaum, H. 1978 *Values Clarification*, 2nd edn. A & W Visual Library, New York.

Appendix

Skills Activities for Developing Communication Skills

Practice is essential if you are to develop the skills described in this book. The activities described here are varied. Some you can work through on your own, some will require that you work with a friend or partner and others are for use in small groups. All of them have been used in a variety of training workshops with different sorts of health care workers.

These activities also contain other details about different aspects of communication. Even if you do not plan to do the activities right now, read through them and reflect on some of the issues that are raised — particularly those concerning cultural aspects of communication. The skilled health care worker needs to pay attention to a whole range of differences in their client's verbal and non-verbal behaviour. It cannot be assumed that what is 'normal' in a Western European context is necessarily the case in others. As a simple example of this social fact, note the different ways that British and American men cross their legs when they sit down! You don't think there is a difference? Try watching a few American films or television programmes and the difference will become noticeable very quickly. Notice, too, differences in 'language styles'. People in different cultures use language differently. Again, compare the British and American use of the word 'fag' as an example of two uses of the same word. Begin to appreciate how important it is to think about the words that you use — particularly when working with clients and colleagues from other cultures.

Skills Activity Number 1

Aim of the Activity
To explore other people's communication skills.

Number of People Required
One.

Description of Activity
Set aside part of a day, perhaps at the weekend. Concentrate, hard, on watching other people communicate in the community around you. Observe people at home, in shops, talking to friends and so forth. Notice what seems to make for *effective* communication and what seems to *inhibit* communication.

Skills Activity Number 2

Aim of the Activity
To explore other professional communication skills.

Number of People Required
One.

Description of Activity
This is rather like the previous activity but is focused on observing people at work. Set aside a short period of time (perhaps a tea-break) and observe people in your work place communicating with others. Notice what works and what doesn't. If you could change certain aspects of people's behaviour, what changes would you make?

Skills Activity Number 3

Aim of the Activity
To explore communication skills used by television interviewers.

Number of People Required
One.

Description of Activity
Find out the time of an 'interview' programme on the television. Watch it and notice the skills used by the interviewer. Compare these with the skills used by television news interviewers. Notice, in particular, the skills used by the interviewers who are 'off camera' — the ones that you do not see but only

hear their voice. Are their skills effective and do you approve of all of the skills they use? What could you learn from television communicators? Is there a difference between the sorts of skills used on television and the sorts of skills you use as a health care worker?

Skills Activity Number 4

Aim of the Activity
To observe salespeople at work.

Number of People Required
One.

Description of Activity
Observe a person serving a customer in a large store. Note their body language and, if you can, the words that they use. Notice, particularly, whether or not they listen to the customer and how they respond. How different is this form of communication to that used in the health care field?

Skills Activity Number 5

Aim of the Activity
To observe non-verbal behaviour.

Number of People Required
One.

Description of Activity
When a play comes on the television, turn the volume right down for a few minutes and observe the non-verbal communication between the actors. To what degree is this sort of non-verbal communication (in acting) different to that in 'real life'?

Skills Activity Number 6

Aim of the Activity
To observe the non-verbal and paralinguistic behaviour of someone using the telephone.

Number of People Required
One.

Description of Activity

Next time someone in your house or in the office uses the phone, pay attention to their non-verbal communication. Note, particularly, whether or not you can work out who is on the other end of the phone. When people talk to each other on the phone, they often 'mirror' each other's tones of voice and their laughter. Notice whether or not you do this.

Skills Activity Number 7

Aim of the Activity
To compare different types of language styles.

Number of People Required
One.

Description of Activity
People use different language styles and different sorts of expressions and vocabularies according to whom they are talking. Compare the language styles of the following types of people:

- a newsreader on the television
- a health care worker talking to a client
- a person talking to another person in a bus queue or other public place
- a person giving directions to another person.

Skills Activity Number 8

Aim of the Activity
To observe different cultural styles of verbal and non-verbal behaviour.

Number of People Required
One.

Description of Activity
You can only do this one when you go on holiday! Observe the way that people in other countries and cultures use language (if you speak it) and use non-verbal communication. Note, particularly, proximity (how close or distant they stand in relation to each other), facial expression and hand gestures. Note, too, whether both people maintain eye contact with each other. It is notable that in some cultures, eye contact is not made by the person who is talking. In other cultures, eye contact is not maintained between junior and senior people when they are talking to each other. Awareness

of cultural differences in communication is an important part of becoming interpersonally skilled.

Skills Activity Number 9

Aim of the Activity
To notice the effects of dress on communication.

Number of People Required
One.

Description of Activity
Try to notice people who do not appear to dress 'appropriately'. For example, I was at an international conference recently and all but one of the male speakers was dressed in a suit and tie. The other one wore jeans and a tee-shirt. The result was that everyone seemed to remember the one who dressed differently! Try to observe the effect on others of a person who does not conform in terms of their dress.

Skills Activity Number 10

Aim of the Activity
To observe different uses of language.

Number of People Required
One.

Description of Activity
Watch an American film and do not follow the plot but listen to the words and phrases that are used. Think about how differently language is used, even though the language, itself — English — is the same. To what degree do *you* use language in a different way to people in other parts of the UK? Try to identify particular styles of talking that can be associated with your part of the country. For example, a frequent greeting in South Wales is 'Hiya!', whereas in the south east of England, a similar greeting might be 'Hi!' or 'Hello!' To what degree is accent linked to particular use of language?

Skills Activity Number 11

Aim of the Activity
To experiment with behaviour (1).

Number of People Required

One.

Description of Activity

For a small part of one day, try to change your behaviour for a little while. If you are normally someone who 'slouches' a little, try holding yourself up very straight. If you talk fairly quietly, try talking loudly. Or if you rarely make eye contact with people you do not know, try looking someone straight in the eye. Notice the effect that this has both on you and on the person with whom you interact. This has been used as a form of therapy for people who have difficulty in communicating. If you like the activity, try it for a longer period. You may be most comfortable changing your behaviour in the company of people who do not know you! To what degree do behaviour habits become ingrained? From whom, or how did you learn *your* behaviour habits? What purpose do they serve? Are you happy with them? Could you change the ones that you do not like, permanently?

Skills Activity Number 12

Aim of the Activity

To experiment with behaviour (2).

Number of People Required

One.

Description of Activity

Next time you are in conversation with a person you know, try to hang back a little before you reply to what they say. See if they then volunteer to say more. This simple exercise can be an interesting way of learning how to listen. On the other hand, it can also be difficult and a little disconcerting.

Skills Activity Number 13

Aim of the Activity

To identify your strengths and deficits in communication.

Number of People Required

One.

Description of Activity

Read through the following items in the box and score each item according to whether you would find communication with the person Easy, Difficult or if you are Unsure.

Item	Easy	Unsure	Difficult
• a person much younger than you • a person much older than you • a person you thought was very like you • a person you thought was very different to you • a person of a different race or culture • a person who was physically very ill • a person who was mentally ill • a person who was mentally handicapped • a person you hardly knew.			

Skills Activity Number 14

Aim of the Activity
To explore personal behaviour.

Number of People Required
Two or multiples of two.

Description of Activity
With a partner, sit opposite one another and give each other feedback about how well each of you communicates. Concentrate only on the positive aspects of the other person's verbal and non-verbal behaviour and give as much feedback as you can. When you have each finished, discuss what it was like to do this activity. If you know each other really well you can also ask to receive negative feedback, but only do this if you choose to. Be careful about offering 'half-hearted' feedback along the lines of: 'I think you smile a lot and that helps you to communicate with others but, I wish you wouldn't . . .' Notice how often or how rarely *you* use 'but' statements in your evaluation of other people. Notice how the 'but' always spoils the positive part of the message. Try to observe other people's use of the 'but' statement, too.

Skills Activity Number 15

Aim of the Activity
To explore personal behaviour.

Number of People Required
Two or multiples of two.

Description of Activity
Sit with a partner in silence. Then, have one of you move the other person into different positions to express different feelings. Alternatively, you might alter the other person's posture, by pressing gently back on their shoulders or by lifting their head a little. Then, once you have 'placed' the person in this way, discuss what that position means to each of you. Repeat the activity by reversing roles.

Skills Activity Number 16

Aim of the Activity
To clarify your communication skills and deficits.

Number of People Required
One.

Description of Activity
Read through the following list of situations and identify whether you could cope with them effectively from the point of view of personal communication. Which of these do you need to do further work on?

Situation	Yes	Unsure	No
• talking to a senior colleague • talking to a person in a shop when you are returning faulty goods • holding a conversation with a client.			

Skills Activity Number 17

Aim of the Activity
To identify your strengths and deficits in the field of communication.

Number of People Required
One.

Description of Activity
Think about your communication skills as they are at present and having read

this book. Write down, in the columns below, your strengths and deficits as a communicator. Which column was easiest to fill in? What are the strengths and deficits that you have *not* jotted down?

My strengths in communication are:	My deficits in communication are:
1.	1.
2.	2.
3.	3.
4.	4.
5.	5.
6.	6.
7.	7.
8.	8.
9.	9.
10.	10.

Now decide what you need to do to rectify the deficits and enhance your strengths even further.

Skills Activity Number 18

Aim of the Activity
To explore the use of non-verbal behaviour.

Number of People Required
Two or multiples of two.

Description of Activity
This is an easy exercise to describe but it can have hilarious and unexpected results. Simply sit with another person and have a 'silent' conversation with them. You may use any non-verbal behaviour you choose, so experiment with expression, gesture, eye contact and so on. When you have carried out this 'conversation' for about five minutes, stop and discuss what each of you thought about the activity.

Skills Activity Number 19

Aim of the Activity
To explore the lack of non-verbal behaviour.

Number of People Required

Two or multiples of two.

Description of Activity

Sit opposite another person and try to hold a conversation that involves as little non-verbal behaviour as possible. Try to keep your gestures and facial expressions to a minimum and limit the range of your tone of voice.

Skills Activity Number 20

Aim of the Activity

To explore total lack of non-verbal behaviour.

Number of People Required

Two or multiples of two.

Description of Activity

Sit with another person and then turn your chairs back-to-back so that you are both facing away from each other. Then, carry out a conversation with each other. Notice what it feels like to have no non-verbal behaviour to observe and notice what difference it makes to your conversation. This is a useful format for learning the telephone counselling skills discussed in the text.

Skills Activity Number 21

Aim of the Activity

To explore communication skills in a group setting.

Number of People Required

Between five and ten people.

Description of Activity

Sit in a closed group. Have each person in turn finish each of the following sentences. Every sentence should be finished before the group moves on to the next. Afterwards, explore the degree to which there were 'patterns' of responses occurring.

- 'I communicate best when . . .'
- 'To improve my communication skills, I need to . . .'
- 'I don't like communicating with . . .'
- 'The easiest person to communicate with is . . .'

Skills Activity Number 22

Aim of the Activity
To explore potential difficulties in communication.

Number of People Required
Between five and ten people.

Description of Activity
Sit in a closed group. Discuss any potential difficulties that group members may anticipate in communicating with the following people in a work context:

- an elderly person
- a person with AIDS
- a young person
- a person who wants to have an abortion
- a person who asks your advice about birth control
- a gay person
- a child
- a person who is dying.

Skills Activity Number 23

Aim of the Activity
To explore silence in a group.

Number of People Required
Between five and ten people.

Description of Activity
Sit in a closed circle and observe the only group rule: to remain totally silent for ten minutes. After that ten minutes, discuss the effects of the silence. Allow for some embarrassed laughter during this exercise.

Skills Activity Number 24

Aim of the Activity
To explore listening in a group.

Number of People Required
Between five and ten people.

Description of Activity

Sit in a closed circle and hold a discussion. Observe the following rule. A person may only contribute to the discussion once they have accurately summarised what the previous speaker has said and to the satisfaction of that previous speaker. This is a useful activity for developing basic counselling skills in a group setting.

Skills Activity Number 25

Aim of the Activity

To explore eye contact in a group.

Number of People Required

Between five and ten people.

Description of Activity

Sit in a closed group and in silence. One person starts the activity by turning to the person on their right and making sustained eye contact. Then, the person on the right slowly turns to the person on his or her right and makes sustained eye contact. This is continued until the 'eye contact' has gone right round the group. Group members are asked to note, particularly, the point at which they decide to break eye contact with one person and to take it up with another. This activity can spark of a lot of discussion about communicating with eye contact. Allow for some nervous laughter with this activity.

Skills Activity Number 26

Aim of the Activity

To experiment with non-verbal communication in a group setting.

Number of People Required

Between five and ten people.

Description of Activity

Sit in a closed group. All of the members spend some time holding a discussion whilst sitting in one of the following positions:

- all group members fold their arms and legs
- all group members avoid making eye contact with other group members
- all group members sit with arms and legs uncrossed

- all group members sit in a slouched position
- all group members sit on the floor.

It is interesting if the group spends about 10 to 15 minutes in each of these positions and then discusses the effect of the activity on the discussion. Also, try to discuss personal preferences and personal reactions to the activity. Group members might like to think up their own variations on this activity.

Skills Activity Number 27

Aim of the Activity
To experience lack of non-verbal communication in a group setting.

Number of People Required
Between five and ten people.

Description of Activity
Sit in a closed group and then have all the group members turn their chairs around so that they are all facing away from each other then hold a discussion for 10 to 15 minutes. Afterwards, have everyone turn their chairs back again and discuss the activity.

Skills Activity Number 28

Aim of the Activity
To explore clear communication in a group.

Number of People Required
Between five and ten people.

Description of Activity
Sit in a closed group. Hold a discussion observing the following 'ground rules':

- Everyone in the group must say 'I' when they are speaking, rather than 'we', 'you' or 'people'. Thus, a person says 'I feel uncomfortable in the group at the moment' rather than 'Sometimes, people feel uncomfortable in groups' or 'You know what it's like, you get to feel uncomfortable.' This ground rule makes sure that people 'own' what they say.
- Everyone in the group speaks directly to another person in the group, thus avoiding expressions such as 'I think what David is trying to say is . . .' In this example, the proper phrase would be 'I think you are trying to say . . .'

- Everyone avoids theorising about what is going on in the group. Thus, statements such as 'It seems to me that the group is avoiding difficult topics' are avoided. Instead, group members focus on what they are thinking and feeling. The discussion stays in the 'here-and-now'.
- Everyone takes some risks in disclosing what they are thinking and feeling.

This is a powerful training exercise in becoming much more clear in communicating with others. The ground rules can, if people want them to, become a way of life. They can also promote more direct and assertive communication.

Skills Activity Number 29

Aim of the Activity
To explore communication.

Number of People Required
Between five and ten people.

Description of Activity
Sit in a closed group and hold a discussion on the topic: 'No one in this group communicates very well'. After about 20 minutes, stop the discussion and discuss the consequences.

Skills Activity Number 30

Aim of the Activity
To identify important elements of communication.

Number of People Required
Between five and ten people.

Description of Activity
This activity involves the use of a flip-chart pad or a blackboard. One person acts as 'scribe' and the group 'brainstorms' on the subject of 'communication'. Group members are asked to call out any words or phrases that they associate with the word. Nothing is edited out by the scribe — even the most unlikely associations are jotted down. After 15 minutes, the brainstorming stops and the group discusses the words. Alternatively, the words can be grouped together under a series of headings that 'emerge' out of the words and phrases.

Skills Activity Number 31

Aim of the Activity
To identify effective communication skills amongst group members.

Number of People Required
Between five and ten people.

Description of Activity
Sit in a closed group. Each person in turn receives positive comments about his or her communication skills from other group members. It is important that only positive things are said and that no 'but' statements are offered. In other words, no one says 'I think that it is important that you always look at people when you talk to them and that you always seem to listen . . . but . . .'

Skills Activity Number 32

Aim of the Activity
To experience a leaderless group.

Number of People Required
Between five and ten people.

Description of Activity
Sit in a closed group. No one is appointed leader and no one takes on the leadership role. For 20 minutes, group members are left to struggle with start-ing and continuing a discussion. After 20 minutes, the usual leader takes over and the group discuss the experience.

Skills Activity Number 33

Aim of the Activity
To keep a personal log of experience.

Number of People Required
One.

Description of Activity
Simply keep a journal of events that happen to you and a log of your develop-ing communication skills. Use the following headings for each day's entry:

● general comments about the day

- aspects of communication that are improving
- aspects of communication that need further work
- names and references of any books or articles read on the topic of communication
- names and references of books or articles to be read
- new communication skills tried or noted
- other comments.

Skills Activity Number 34

Aim of the Activity
To explore personal boundaries in communication.

Number of People Required
One.

Description of Activity
Read through the following items and consider the degree to which you could discuss the items with another person. Tick Easy, Difficult or Don't Know in the columns provided.

Item	Easy	Don't know	Difficult
1. my feelings 2. my financial situation 3. my prejudices 4. my sexuality 5. my fears 6. my schooldays 7. my hopes for the future 8. my political views 9. my dislikes 10. my good qualities 11. my bad habits 12. the worst things about me 13. why people like me			

What were the most difficult things to think about discussing with another person? Who *could* you discuss those things with? To what degree do we expect clients to discuss these sorts of things with us?

Skills Activity Number 35

Aim of the Activity
To identify qualities that you look for in other people.

Number of People Required
One.

Description of Activity
Read through the following list of qualities and classify them according to which ones you look for in another person. Use the following codes: Essential, Don't know, Not important.

Quality	Essential	Don't know	Not important
1. ability to listen			
2. generosity			
3. sense of humour			
4. similar views to mine			
5. different views to mine			
6. likeable			
7. warm			
8. quiet			
9. honest			
10. outgoing			
11. talkative			
12. creative			
13. exciting			
14. stands out from the crowd			
15. ordinary			
16. temperamental			

Now read through the list again, and put a cross in each box according to whether or not you think *you* have those qualities. Put a cross against the qualities that you have. Then compare the qualities you look for in another person with the qualities that you think you have yourself.

Skills Activity Number 36

Aim of the Activity
To explore non-verbal aspects of speech

Number of People Required
Two or multiples of two.

Description of Activity
Sit opposite the other person and then hold five-minute conversations observing the following rules. After each five-minute conversation, you move on to the next rule.

Rule One
One person speaks very quietly whilst the other speaks normally.
Rule Two
Both people speak very quietly.
Rule Three
One person raises their voice.
Rule Four
Both people raise their voices.
Rule Five
Both people sit three yards apart.
Rule Six
Both people sit with knees almost touching.
Rule Seven
One person avoids all eye contact during the conversation.
Rule Eight
Both people avoid all eye contact during the conversation.

Skills Activity Number 37

Aim of the Activity
To explore aspects of assertiveness.

Number of People Required
Two or multiples of two.

Description of Activity
Sit opposite the other person. Then, one person says 'no', whilst the other person answers 'yes'. Repeat this 'yes' and 'no' over and over again, experimenting with different tones of voice and different sorts of non-verbal communication. Afterwards, try to describe your feelings about the experience.

Skills Activity Number 38

Aim of the Activity
To experience loss of one sense.

Number of People Required
Two or multiples of two.

Description of Activity
This is the well known 'blind walk' activity. One of you wears a blindfold (or keeps his or her eyes closed at all times) whilst the other leads the blindfolded person around. Try to make sure that the person is taken into different rooms, different parts of the building and, at some point, outside the building. Afterwards, discuss your feelings about the experience.

Skills Activity Number 39

Aim of the Activity
To enhance communication awareness.

Number of Persons Required
One.

Description of Activity
Develop the habit of 'noticing'. This is to say, keep your attention focused 'out', as described in the text. Stay awake and concentrate on things that are going on around you. Notice people and make it a habit to observe them. Observe, too, your own behaviour and your own development as a communicator. In the end, it becomes obvious that it becomes a fascinating and lifelong process.

The golden rules of effective communication

This is the end of the book. Now, the hard work starts. You have to notice your own communication skills in action, diagnose what you need to work on and then practice the new skills. To close, here is a summary of the essential rules of effective communication for any health care setting:

● Learn to listen more carefully — this is the key to caring communication.
● Communicate clearly and simply. Try to say exactly what you mean and avoid long words and jargon.

- Practice. Communication is a skill. Like all others, it improves with practice.
- Seek feedback. Ask other people to assess your skills. Listen to what they say and then decide whether or not you need to act.
- Continue to notice your own and others' communication skills. Communication skills are not 'once and for all', they are changing all the time, just as the culture and society is changing all the time. In the end, though, people stay people and it is with people that we communicate. Keep at it and good luck.

Bibliography

These are books on communication that you may find useful in furthering your study of the topic. Remember that if you cannot find them in your local college or public library, it may be possible to get them through the Inter-Library Loan system. Ask your librarian.

Remember to keep a reference card for each book that you read so that you can refer to it again in the future.

Adler, R.B. 1977 *Confidence in Communication: A Guide to Assertive Social Skills.* Holt, Rinehart and Winston, London.

Adler, R. and Rodman, G. 1988 *Understanding Human Communication,* 3rd edn. Holt, Rinehart and Winston, New York.

Adler, R.B. and Towne, N. 1984 *Looking Out/Looking In: Interpersonal Communication.* Holt Rinehart and Winston, London.

Adler, R.B., Rosenfield, L.B. and Towne, N. 1983 *Interplay: The Process of Interpersonal Communication.* Holt, Rinehart and Winston, London.

Alberti, R.E. and Emmons, M.L. 1982 *Your Perfect Right: A Guide to Assertive Living,* 4th edn. Impact Publishers, San Luis, California.

Allan, J. 1989 *How to Develop Your Personal Management Skills.* Kogan Page, London.

Argyle, M (ed) 1981 *Social Skills and Health.* Methuen, London.

Argyle, M. 1983 *The Psychology of Interpersonal Behaviour,* 4th edn. Penguin, Harmondsworth, Middlesex.

Argyris, C. 1982 *Reasoning, Learning and Action.* Jossey Bass, San Francisco.

Argyris, C. and Schon, D. 1974 *Theory in Practice: Increasing Professional Effectiveness.* Jossey Bass, San Francisco.

Arnold, E. and Boggs, K. 1989 *Interpersonal Relationships: Professional Communication Skills for Nurses.* Saunders, Philadelphia.

Atwood, A.H. 1979 The mentor in clinical practice. *Nursing Outlook,* **27**, 714–17.

Ausberger, D. 1979 *Anger and Assertiveness in Pastoral Care.* Fortress Press, Philadelphia.

Baddeley, D. 1983 *Your Memory: A User's Guide.* Penguin, Harmondsworth, Middlesex.

Baer, J. 1976 *How to Be Assertive (Not Aggressive): Women in Life, in Love and on the Job.* Signet, New York.

Bailey, R 1985 *Coping With Stress in Caring*. Blackwell, Oxford.

Ball, M.J. and Hannah, K.J. 1984 *Using Computers in Nursing*. Reston Publishing, Reston, Virginia.

Baruth, L.G. 1987 *An Introduction to the Counselling Profession*. Prentice Hall, Englewood Cliffs, New Jersey.

Belkin, G.S. 1984 *Introduction to Counselling*. Brown, Dubuque, Iowa.

Bellack, A.S. and Hersen, M (eds) 1979 *Research and Practice in Social Skills Training*. Plenum Press, New York.

Benner, P. and Wrubel, J. 1989 *The Primacy of Caring: Stress and Coping in Health and Illness*. Addison Wesley, Menlo Park.

Bolger, A.W. (ed) 1982 *Counselling in Britain: A Reader*. Batsford Academic, London.

Bond, M. and Kilty, J. 1986 *Practical Methods of Dealing With Stress*, 2nd edn. Human Potential Research Project, University of Surrey, Guildford.

Boud, D.J. (ed) *Developing Student Autonomy in Learning*. Kogan Page, London.

Boud, D. and Prosser, M.T. 1980 Sharing responsibility: staff–student cooperation in learning. *British Journal of Educational Technology*, **11 (1)**, 24–35.

Boud, D., Keogh, R. and Walker, M. 1985 *Reflection: Turning Experience into Learning*. Kogan Page, London.

Bower, S.A. and Bower, G.H. 1976 *Asserting Yourself*. Addison Wesley, Reading, Massachusetts.

Boydel, E.M. and Fales, A.W. 1983 Reflective learning: key to learning from experience. *Journal of Humanistic Psychology*, **23 (2)**, 99–117.

Brandes, D. and Phillips, R. 1984 *The Gamester's Handbook*, vol 2. Hutchinson, London.

Brasweel, M. and Seay, T. 1984 *Approaches to Counselling and Psychotherapy*. Waverly, Prospect Heights, California.

Brookfield, S.D. 1986 *Understanding and Facilitating Adult Learning: A Comprehensive Analysis of Principles and Effective Practices*. Open University Press, Milton Keynes.

Brookfield, S.D. 1987 *Developing Critical Thinkers: Challenging Adults to Explore Alternative Ways of Thinking and Acting*. Open University Press, Milton Keynes.

Broome, A. 1990 *Managing Change*. Macmillan, London.

Brown, A. 1979 *Groupwork*. Heinemann, London.

Brown, S.D. and Lent, R.W. (eds) 1984 *Handbook of Counselling Psychology*. Wiley, Chichester.

Brown, D. and Srebalus, D.J. 1988 *An Introduction to the Counselling Process*. Prentice Hall, Philadelphia.

Burnard, P. 1984 Developing self-awareness. *Nursing Mirror*, **158 (21)**, 30–1.

Burnard, P. 1984 Training to be aware. *Senior Nurse*, **1 (23)**, 25–7.

Burnard, P. 1985 Listening to People. *Nursing Mirror*, **16 (18)**, 28–9.

Burnard, P. 1985 Learning to communicate. *Nursing Mirror*, **16 (19)**, 30–1.

Burnard, P. 1985 How to reduce stress. *Nursing Mirror*, **16 (19)**, 47–8.

Burnard, P. 1986 Encountering adults. *Senior Nurse*, **4 (4)**, 30-1.

Burnard, P. 1986 Learning about groups. *Nurse Education Today*, **6**, 116–20.

Burnard, P. 1986 Integrated self-awareness training: a holistic model. *Nurse Education Today*, **6**, 219–22.

Burnard, P. 1987 Coping with emotion in intensive care nursing. *Intensive Care Nursing*, **3 (4)**, 157–9.

Burnard, P. 1987 Meaningful dialogue. *Nursing Times*, **83 (20)**, 43–5.

Burnard, P. 1987 Self and peer assessment. *Senior Nurse*, **6 (5)**, 16–17.

Burnard, P. 1987 Counselling: basic principles in nursing. *The Professional Nurse*, **2 (9)**, 278–80.

Burnard, P. 1987 The right direction. *Senior Nurse*, **7 (1)**, 30–2.

Burnard, P. 1987 The health visitor as counsellor: a framework for interpersonal skills. *Health Visitor*, **60 (8)**, 269.

Burnard, P. 1987 Interpersonal skills: sharing a viewpoint. *Senior Nurse*, **7 (3)**, 38–9.

Burnard, P. 1987 Developing skills as a group facilitator. *The Professional Nurse*, **3 (1)**, 19–21.

Burnard, P. 1987 Teaching the teachers. *Nursing Times*, **83 (49)**, 63–5.

Burnard, P. 1987 Counselling skills. *Journal of District Nursing*, **6 (7)**, 12–14.

Burnard, P. 1987 Learning to listen. *Journal of District Nursing*, **6 (9)**, 26–8.

Burnard, P. 1988 Communicating on the telephone. *Senior Nurse*, **8 (13)**, 14–18.

Burnard, P. 1988 Self-awareness. *Journal of District Nursing*, **6 (10)**, 27–9.

Burnard, P. 1988 Emotional release. *Journal of District Nursing*, **6 (11)**, 26–8.

Burnard, P. 1988 Developing counselling skills in health visitors: an experiential approach. *Health Visitor*, **61 (5)**, 20–3.

Burnard, P. 1988 Building on experience. *Senior Nurse*, **8 (5)**, 18–20.

Burnard, P. 1988 Four dimensions in counselling. *Nursing Times*, **84 (20)**, 37–9.

Burnard, P. 1988 Searching for meaning. *Nursing Times*, **84 (37)**, 34–6.

Burnard, P. 1988 AIDS and sexuality. *Journal of District Nursing*, **7 (2)**, 7–8.

Burnard, P. 1988 Empathy: the key to understanding. *The Professional Nurse*, **3 (10)**, 388–92.

Burnard, P. 1988 Self-directed learning. *Journal of District Nursing*, **7 (1)**, 7–8.

Burnard, P. 1988 Coping with other people's emotions. *The Professional Nurse*, **4 (1)**, 11–14.

Burnard, P. 1988 Preventing burnout. *Journal of District Nursing*, **7 (5)**, 9–10.

Burnard, P. 1988 Mentors: a supporting act. *Nursing Times*, **84 (46)**, 27–8.

Burnard, P. 1988 Discussing spiritual issues with clients. *Health Visitor*, **61 (12)**, 371–2.

Burnard, P. 1988 The spiritual needs of atheists and agnostics. *The Professional Nurse*, **4 (3)**, 130–2.

Burnard, P. 1988 Stress and relaxation in health visiting. *Health Visitor*, **61 (12)**, 272.

Burnard, P. 1988 The heart of the counselling relationship. *Senior Nurse*, **8 (12)**, 17–18.

Burnard, P. 1988 Equality and meaning: issues in the interpersonal relationship. *Community Psychiatric Nursing Journal*, **8 (6)**, 17–21.

Burnard, P. 1988 The journal as an assessment and evaluation tool in nurse education. *Nurse Education Today*, **8**, 105–7.

Burnard, P. 1988 Self evaluation methods in nurse education. *Nurse Education Today*, **8**, 229–33.

Burnard, P. 1988 Self-awareness and intensive care nursing. *Intensive Care Nursing*, **4** 67–70

Burnard, P. 1988 Experiential learning: some theoretical considerations. *International Journal of Lifelong Education*, **7 (2)**, 127–33.

Burnard, P. 1988 'Brainstorming': a practical learning activity in nurse education. *Nurse Education Today*, **8**, 354–8.

Burnard, P. 1989 Psychiatric nursing students' perceptions of experiential learning. *Nursing Times*, **85 (1)**, 52.

Burnard, P. 1989 The role of mentor. *Journal of District Nursing*, **8 (3)**, 8–10.

Burnard, P. 1989 Exploring sexuality. *Journal of District Nursing*, **8 (4)**, 9–11.

Burnard, P. 1989 Counselling in surgical nursing. *Surgical Nurse*, **2 (5)**, 12–14.

Burnard, P. 1989 Exploring nurses' attitudes to AIDS. *The Professional Nurse*, **5 (2)**, 84–90.

Burnard, P. 1989 Learning from the learners. *Nursing Standard*, **4 (6),** 26–7.

Burnard, P. 1989 The 'sixth sense'. *Nursing Times*, **85 (50)**, 52–3.

Burnard, P. 1989 *Teaching Interpersonal Skills: An Experiential Handbook for Health Professionals*. Chapman and Hall, London.

Burnard, P. 1990 *Learning Human Skills: An Experiential Guide for Nurses*. 2nd edn. Heinemann, Oxford.

Burnard, P. 1990 Counselling the boss. *Nursing Times*, **86 (1)**, 58–9.

Burnard, P. 1990 Counselling in crises. *Journal of District Nursing*, **8 (7)**, 15–16

Burnard, P. 1990 Learning to care for the spirit. *Nursing Standard*, **4 (18)**, 38–9.

Burnard, P. 1990 Recording counselling in nursing. *Senior Nurse*, **10 (3)**, 26–7.

Burnard, P. 1990 Critical awareness in nurse education. *Nursing Standard*, **4 (30)**, 32–4.

Burnard, P. 1990 The supervisory role. *Journal of District Nursing*, **July**, 26–7.

Burnard, P. 1990 Group discussion. *Nursing Times*, **12 (86)**, 36–7.

Burnard, P. 1990 Using experiental teaching methods. *Nursing Times*, **86 (41)**, 53.

Burnard, P. 1990 So you think you need a computer? *The Professional Nurse*, **6 (2)**, 119–20.

Burnard, P. 1990 Exploring meaninglessness. *Journal of District Nursing*, **9 (6)**, 10–13.

Burnard, P. 1991 Computing: an aid to studying nursing. *Nursing Standard*, **5 (17)**, 36–8.

Burnard, P. 1991 Exploring personal values. *Journal of District Nursing*, **9 (7)**, 7–8.

Burnard, P. 1991 Peer support groups. *Journal of District Nursing*, **9 (8)**, 19–20.

Burnard, P. 1991 Perceptions of experiental learning. *Nursing Times*, **87 (8)**, 47.

Burnard, P. 1991 Interpersonal skills training. *Journal of District Nursing*, **9 (10)**, 17–20.

Burnard, P. 1991 Improving through reflection. *Journal of District Nursing*, **9 (11)**, 10–12.

Burnard, P. 1991 Assertiveness and clinical practice. *Nursing Standard*, **5 (33)**, 37–9.

Burnard, P. 1991 Using video as a reflective tool in interpersonal skills training. *Nurse Education Today*, **11**, 143–6.

Burnard, P. and Morrison, P. 1987 Nurses' perceptions of their interpersonal skills. *Nursing Times*, **83 (42)**, 59.

Burnard, P. and Morrison, P. 1989 Counselling attitudes in community psychiatric nurses. *Community Psychiatric Nursing Journal*, **9 (5)**, 26–9.

Burnard, P. and Morrison, P. 1990 Psychological aspects of self-esteem. *Surgical Nurse*, **3 (4)**, 4–6.

Burnard, P. and Morrison, P. 1990 Counselling attitudes in health visiting students. *Health Visitor*, **63 (11)**, 389–90.

Calnan, J. 1983 *Talking with Patients*. Heinemann, London.

Campbell, A.V. 1981 *Rediscovering Pastoral Care*. Darton, Longman and Todd, London.

Campbell, A. 1984 *Moderated Love*. SPCK, London.

Campbell, A. 1984 *Paid to Care?* SPCK, London.

Carcuff, R.R. 1969 *Helping and Human Relations, vol I: selection and training*. Holt, Rinehart and Winston, New York.

Carlisle, J. and Leary, M. 1982 Negotiating groups. In Payne, R. and Cooper. C. (eds) *Groups at Work*. Wiley, Chichester.

Chenevert, M. 1978 *Special Techniques in Assertiveness Training for Women in the Health Professions*. CV Mosby, St Louis.

Clark, C. 1978 *Assertive Skills for Nurses*. Contemporary Publishing, Wakefield, Massachusetts.

Claxton, G. 1984 *Live and Learn: An Introduction to the Pyschology of Growth and Change in Everyday Life*. Harper and Row, London.

Collins, G.C. and Scott, P. 1979 Everyone who makes it has Mentor. *Harvard Business Review*, **56,** 89–101.

Corey, F. 1983 *I Never Knew I Had a Choice*, 2nd edn. Brookes-Cole, California.

Cormier, L.S. 1987 *The Professional Counsellor: A Process Guide to Helping*. Prentice Hall, Englewood Cliffs, New Jersey.

Curran, J. and Monti, P. (eds) *Social Skills Training: A Practical Handbook for Assessment and Treatment*. Guildford, New York.

Daniels, V. and Horowitz, L.J. 1984 *Being and Caring: A Psychology for Living*, 2nd edn. Mayfield, Mountain View, California.

Davis, C.M. 1981 Affective education for the health professions. *Physical Therapy*, **61 (11)**, 1587–93.

Dawley, H. and Wenrich, W. 1986 *Achieving Assertive Behaviour: a Guide to Assertive Training*. Brooks/Cole, Monterey, California.

de Bono, E. 1982 *de Bono's Thinking Course*. BBC, London.

De Vito, J.A. 1986 *The Interpersonal Communication Book*, 4th edn. Harper and Row, New York.

deLeeuw, M. and de Leeuw, E. 1965 *Read Better Read Faster*. Penguin, Harmondsworth, Middlesex.

Dickson, A. 1985 *A Woman in Your Own Right: Assertiveness and You*. Quartet Books, London.

Dickson, D.N. and Glover, J.A. 1984 *Counselling: a problem solving approach*. Wiley, Chichester.

Dobson, C.B. 1982 *Stress: The Hidden Anxiety*. MTP Press, Lancaster.

Douglas, T. 1976 *Groupwork Practice*. Tavistock, London.

Dowd, C. 1983 Learning through experience. *Nursing Times*, **27th July,** 50–2.

Dryden, W., Charles-Edwards and Woolfe, R. 1989 *Handbook of Counselling in Britain*. Routledge, London.

Duncan, S. and Fiske, D.W. 1977 *Face-to-Face Interaction: Research, Methods and Theory*. Lawrence Erlbaum Associates, Hillsdale, New Jersey.

Eden, D. 1982 Critical job events, acute stress and strain. *Organisational Behaviour and Human Performance*, **30,** 312–29.

Egan, G. 1986 *Exercises in Helping Skills*, 3rd edn. Brooks/Cole, Monterey, California.

Ellis, R. (ed) 1989 *Professional Competence and Quality Assurance in the Caring Professions*. Chapman and Hall, London.

Ellis, R. and Whittington, D. 1981 *A Guide to Social Skill Training*. Croom Helm, London.

Ernst, S. and Goodison, L. 1981 *In our Own Hands: a Book of Self Help Therapy*. The Women's Press, London.

Evans, D. (ed) 1990 *Why Should We Care?* Macmillan, London.

Fay, A. 1978 *Making Things Better by Making Them Worse*. Hawthorne, New York.

Feldenkrais, M. 1972 *Awareness Through Movement*. Harper and Row, New York.

Fernando, S. 1990. *Mental Health, Race and Culture*. Macmillan, London.

Ferruci, P. 1982 *What We May Be*. Turnstone Press, Wellingborough, Northamptonshire.

Fielding, P. and Berman, P. (eds) 1989 *Surviving in General Management*. Macmillan, London.

Filley, A.C. 1975 *Interpersonal Conflict Resolution*. Scott, Foresman, Glenview, Illinois.

Fineman, S. 1985 *Social Work Stress and Intervention*. Gower, London.

Firth, J. 1985 Personal meanings of occupational stress: cases from the clinic. *Journal of Occupational Psychology*, **58**, 139–48.

Fisher, S. *Stress and Strategy*. Lawrence Erlbaum Associates, London.

Fisher, S. and Reason, J. 1988 *Handbook of Life Stress: Cognition and Health*. Wiley, Chichester.

Fisher, R. and Ury, W. 1983 *Getting to Yes: Negotiating Agreement Without Giving In*. Hutchinson, London.

Foggo-Pays, E 1983 *An Introductory Guide to Counselling*. Ravenswood, Beckenham.

Fontana, D. 1989 *Managing Stress*. British Psychological Society and Routledge, London.

Francis, D. and Young, D. 1979 *Improving Work Groups: A Practical Manual for Team Building*. University Associates, San Diego, California.

Freeman, R. 1982 *Mastering Study Skills*. Macmillan, London.

French, P. 1983 *Social Skills for Nursing Practice*. Croom Helm, London.

Freudenberger, H. and Richelson, G. 1974 *Burnout: How to Beat the High Cost of Success*. Bantam Books, New York.

Gibbs, G. 1981 *Teaching Students to Learn*. Open University, Milton Keynes.

Gibson, R.L. and Mitchell, M.H. 1986 *Introduction to Counselling and Guidance*. Collier Macmillan, London.

Glennerster, H. and Owens, P. 1990 *Nursing in Conflict*. Macmillan, London.

Goffman, I. 1971 *The Presentation of Self in Everyday Life*. Penguin, Harmondsworth, Middlesex.

Goldberg, L and Beznitz, S. 1982 *Handbook of Stress: Theoretical and Clinical Aspects*. Macmillan, New York.

Graham, N.M. 1988 Psychological stress as a public health problem: how much do we know? *Community Health Studies*, **12 (2),** 151–60.

Hanks, L, Belliston, L. and Edwards, D. 1977 *Design Yourself.* Kaufman, Los Altos, California.

Hanson, P. 1986 *The Joy of Stress.* Pan, London.

Hargie, O. (ed) 1987 *A Handbook of Communication Skills.* Croom Helm, London.

Hargie, O., Saunders, C. and Dickson, D. 1981 *Social Skills in Interpersonal Communication,* 2nd edn. Croom Helm, London.

Harris, T. 1969 *I'm OK, You're OK.* Harper and Row, London.

Hawkins, P. and Shohet, R. 1989 *Supervision and the Helping Professions.* Open University Press, Milton Keynes.

Herinck, R. (ed) 1980 *The Psychotherapy Handbook.* New American Library, New York.

Heron, J. 1973 *Experimental Training Techniques.* Human Potential Research Project, University of Surrey, Guildford.

Heron, J. 1977 *Catharsis in Human Development.* Human Potential Research Project, University of Surrey, Guildford.

Heron, J. 1977 *Behaviour Analysis in Education and Training.* Human Potential Research Project, University of Surrey, Guildford.

Heron, J. 1978 *Co-Counselling Teachers Manual.* Human Potential Research Project, University of Surrey, Guildford.

Heywood-Jones, I. 1989 *Helping Hands.* Macmillan, London.

Hill, S.S. and Howlett, H.A. 1988 *Success in Practical Nursing in Personal Vocational Issues.* W.B. Saunders, Philadelphia.

Holt, R. 1982 An alternative to mentorship. *Adult Education.* **55 (2),** 152–6.

Howard, K. and Sharp, J.A. 1983 *The Management of a Student Research Project.* Gower, Aldershot.

Howard, G.S., Nance, D.W. and Meyers, P. 1987 *Adaptive Counselling and Therapy: a systematic approach to selecting effective treatments.* Jossey Bass, San Francisco, California.

Hull, D. and Schroeder, H. 1979 Some interpersonal effects of assertion, non-assertion and aggression. *Behaviour Therapy,* **10,** 20–9.

Hurding, R.F. 1985 *Roots and Shoots: a guide to counselling and psychotherapy.* Hodder and Stoughton, London.

Hutchins, D.E. 1987 *Helping Relationships and Strategies.* Brooks-Cole, Monterey, California.

Ivey, A.E. 1987 *Counselling and Psychotherapy: Skills, theories and practice.* Prentice Hall International, London.

James, M. and Jongeward, D. 1971 *Born to Win: Transactional Analysis with Gestalt Experiments.* Addison-Wesley, Reading, Massachusetts.

Jenkins, E. 1987 *Facilitating Self-Awareness: A Learning Package Combining Group work with Computer Assisted Learning.* Open Software Library, Wigan.

Johnson, D.W. 1972 *Reaching Out.* Prentice Hall, Englewood Cliffs, New Jersey.

Johnson, D.W. and Johnson, F.P. 1982 *Joining Together,* 2nd edn. Prentice Hall, Englewood Cliffs, New Jersey.

Jourard, S. 1964 *The Transparent Self.* Van Nostrand, Princeton, New Jersey.

Jourard, S. 1971 *Self-Disclosure: An Experimental Analysis of the Transparent Self.* Wiley, New York.

Jung, C.G. 1976 *Modern Man in Search of a Soul*. Routledge and Kegan Paul, London.

Kelly, C. 1979 *Assertion Training: A Facilitator's Guide*. University Associates, La Jolla, California.

Kennedy, E. 1979 *On Becoming a Counsellor*. Gill and Macmillan, London.

Kilty, J. 1978 *Self and Peer Assessment*. Human Potential Research Project, University of Surrey, Guildford.

Kilty, J. 1987 *Staff Development for Nurse Education: Practitioner Supporting Students: A Report of a 5-Day Development Workshop*. Human Potential Research Project, University of Surrey, Guildford.

King, E.C. 1984 *Affective Education in Nursing: A Guide to Teaching and Assessment*. Aspen, Maryland.

Kizer, W.M. 1987 *The Health Workplace: A Blueprint for Corporate Action*. Delmar, London.

Koberg, D. and Bagnal, J. 1981 *The Revised All New Universal Traveller: A Soft-Systems Guide to Creativity, Problem-Solving and the Process of Reaching Goals*. Kaufmann, Los Altos, California.

Kopp, S. 1974 *If You Meet the Buddha on the Road, Kill Him! A Modern Pilgrimage Through Myth, Legend and Psychotherapy*. Sheldon Press, London.

Kottler, J.A. and Brown, R.W. 1985 *Introduction to Therapeutic Counselling*. Brooks-Cole, Monterey, California.

L'Abate, L. and Milan, M. (eds) 1985 *Handbook of Social Skills Training and Research*. Wiley, New York.

Lachman, V.D. 1983 *Stress Management, A Manual for Nurses*. Grune and Stratton, Orlando, Florida.

Lang, A.J. and Jakubowski, P. 1978 *The Assertive Option*. Research Press, Champagne.

Larson, D.G. 1986 Developing effective hospice staff support groups: pilot test of an innovative training programs *Hospice Journal*, **2 (2)**, 41–55.

Lazarus, R.S. and Folkman, S. 1984 *Stress, Appraising and Coping*. Springer, New York.

Leady, N.K. 1989 A physiological analysis of stress and chronic illness. *Journal of Advanced Nursing*, **14 (10)**, 868–76.

Leech, K. 1986 *Spirituality and Pastoral Care*. Sheldon Press, London.

Lennon, M.C. 1989 The structural contexts of stress: an invited response of Pearlin. *Journal of Health and Social Behaviour*, **L 30 (3)**, 261-8.

Lewis, M. 1987 *Writing to Win*. McGraw Hill, London.

Lewis, H. and Streitfield, H. 1971 *Growth Games*. Bantam Books, New York.

Liberman, R.P., King, L.W., DeRisi, W.J. and McCann, M. 1976 *Personal Effectiveness*. Research Press, Champagne.

Luft, J. 1984 *Group Processes: An Introduction to Group Dynamics*, 2nd edn. Mayfield, San Francisco.

Lyon, B.L. and Werner, J.S. 1987 Research on Nursing Practice: Stress. *Annual Review of Nursing Research*, **5 (3)**, 22.

Madders, J. 1980 *Stress and Relaxation*. Martin Dunitz, London.

Marshall, E.K. and Kurtz, P.D. (eds) 1982 *Interpersonal Helping Skills: A guide to Training Methods, Programs and Resources*. Jossey Bass, San Francisco, California.

Marson S, (ed) 1990 *Managing People*. Macmillan, London.

McGuire, J. and Priestley, P. 1981 *Life After School: A Social Skills Curriculum.* Pergamon, Oxford.

McIntee, J. and Firth, H. 1984 How to Beat the Burnout. *Health and Social Services Journal,* **9th February**, 166-8.

Meichenbaum, D. 1983 *Coping With Stress.* Century Publishing, London.

Meichenbaum, D. and Jaremko, M.E. 1983 *Stress Reduction and Prevention.* Plenum Press, New York.

Meyeroff, M. 1972 *On Caring.* Harper and Row, New York.

Moore, D. 1977 *Assertive Behaviour: An Annotated Bibliography.* Impact, San Luis Obispo, California.

Moreno, J.L. 1959 *Psychodrama,* vol II. Beacon House Press, Beacon, New York.

Moreno, J.L. 1969 *Psychodrama,* vol III. Beacon House Press, Beacon, New York.

Moreno, J.L. 1977 *Psychodrama,* vol I, 4th edn. Beacon House Press, Beacon, New York.

Morley, I.E. 1982 Preparation for negotiating, conflict, commitment and choice. In Bradstatter, H., Davis, J.H. and Stocker-Kreichgauer, G. (eds) *Group Decision Making.* Academic Press, London.

Morley, I.E. 1987 Negotiating and bargaining. In Hargie, O. (ed) *A Handbook of Communication Skills.* Croom Helm, London.

Morrison, P. and Burnard, P. 1990 Interpersonal skills: a smallest space analysis. *Nursing Times,* **86 (14)**, 55.

Morsund, J. 1985 *The Process of Counselling and Therapy.* Prentice Hall, Englewood Cliffs, New Jersey.

Morton-Cooper, A. 1989 *Returning to Nursing: A Guide for Nurses and Health Visitors.* Macmillan, London.

Munro, A., Manthei, B. and Small, J. 1988. *Counselling: The Skills of Problem-Solving.* Routledge, London.

Murgatroyd, S. 1986 *Counselling and Helping.* British Psychological Society and Methuen, London.

Murgatroyd, S. and Woolfe, R. 1982 *Coping with Crisis—Understanding and Helping Persons in Need.* Harper and Row, London.

Myerscough, P.R. 1989 *Talking With Patients: A Basic Clinical Skill.* Oxford Medical Publications, Oxford.

Nadler, L. (ed) 1984 *The Handbook of Human Resource Development.* Wiley, New York.

Nelson, M.J. 1989 *Managing Health Professionals.* Chapman and Hall, London.

Nelson-Jones, R. 1981 *The Theory and Practice of Counselling Psychology.* Holt Rinehart and Winston, London.

Nelson-Jones, R. 1984 *Personal Responsibility: counselling and therapy: an integrative approach.* Harper and Row, London.

Nelson-Jones, R. 1988 *Practical Counselling and Helping Skills: helping clients to help themselves.* Cassell, London.

Nichols, K. and Jenkinson, J. 1990 *Leading a Support Group.* Chapman and Hall, London.

Nierenberg, G.I. 1973 *Fundamentals of Negotiation.* Hawthorn, New York.

Ohlsen, A.M., Horne, A.M. and Lawe, C.F. 1988 *Group Counselling*. Holt Rinehart and Winston, New York.

Open University Coping With Crisis Group 1987 *Running Workshops: A Guide for Trainers in the Helping Professions*. Croom Helm, London.

Osborn, S.M. and Harris, G.G. 1975 *Assertive Training for Women*. Charles C. Thomas, Springfield, Illinois.

Palmer, M.E. and Deck, E.S. 1982 Assertiveness education: one method for teaching staff and patients. *Nurse Educator*, **Winter**, 36–9.

Payne, R. and Firth-Conzens, J. (eds) 1987 *Stress in Health Professionals*. Wiley, Chichester.

Peplau, H.E. 1988 *Interpersonal Relationships in Nursing*. Macmillan, London.

Phelps, S. and Austin, N. 1975 *The Assertive Woman*, Impact, San Luis Obispo, California.

Phillip-Jones, L. 1982 *Mentors and Proteges*. Arbour House, New York.

Phillip-Jones, L. 1983 Establishing a formalised mentoring programme. *Training and Development Journal*, **February**, 38-42.

Pollack, K. 1988 On the nature of social stress: production of a modern mythology. *Social Science and Medicine*, **26 (3)**, 381–92.

Pope, B. 1986 *Social Skills Training for Psychiatric Nurses*. Harper and Row, London.

Porritt, L. 1990 *Interaction Strategies: An Introduction for Health Professionals*, 2nd edn. Churchill Livingstone, Edinburgh.

Priestley, P., McQuire, J., Flegg, D., Hemsley, V. and Welham, D. 1978 *Social Skills and Personal Problem Solving*. Tavistock, London.

The Professional Nurse Developments Series 1990 *The Ward Sister's Survival Guide*. Austen Cornish, London.

The Professional Nurse Developments Series 1990 *Practice Check!* Austen Cornish, London.

The Professional Nurse Developments Series 1990 *Effective Communicating*. Austen Cornish, London.

The Professional Nurse Developments Series 1990 *Patient Education Plus*. Austen Cornish, London.

The Professional Nurse Developments Series 1990 *The Staff Nurse's Survival Guide*. Austen Cornish, London.

Rankin-Box, D.F. 1987 *Complementary Health Therapies: A Guide for Nurses and the Caring Professions*. Chapman and Hall, London.

Rawlings, M.E. and Rawlings, L. 1983 Mentoring and networking for helping professionals. *Personnel and Guidance Journal*, **62 (2),** 116–18.

Reddy, M. 1987 *The Manager's Guide to Counselling at Work*. Methuen, London.

Roche, G.R. 1979 Much Ado About Mentors. *Harvard Business Review*, **56**, 14–28.

Rogers, C.R. 1951 *Client-Centred Therapy*. Constable, London.

Rogers, C.R. 1967 *On Becoming a Person*. Constable, London.

Rogers, J.C. 1982 Sponsorship—developing leaders for occupational therapy. *American Journal of Occupational Therapy*, **36**, 309–13.

Rogers, J.C. and Dodson, S.C. 1988 Burnout in occupational therapists. *American Journal of Occupational Therapy*, **42 (12)**, 787–92.

Rogers, C.R. and Stevens, B. 1967 *Person to Person: The Problem of Being Human*. Real People Press, Lafayette, California.

Russell, P. 1979 *The Brain Book*. Routledge and Kegan Paul, London.

Scammell, B. 1990 *Communication Skills*. Macmillan, London.

Schmidt, J.A. and Wolfe, J.S. 1980 The mentor partnership: discovery of professionalism. *NASPA Journal*, **17**, 45–51.

Schon, D.A. 1983 *The Reflective Practitioner: How Professionals Think in Action*. Basic Books, New York.

Schorr, T.M. 1978 The Lost Art of Mentoring. *American Journal of Nursing*, **78**, 1873.

Schulman, D. 1982 *Intervention in Human Services: A guide to skills and knowledge*, 3rd edn. CV Mosby, St Louis.

Scott, W.P. 1986 *The Skills of Communicating*. Gower, Aldershot.

Shafer, P. 1978 *Humanistic Psychology*. Prentice Hall, Englewood Cliffs, New Jersey.

Shapiro, E.C., Haseltime, F, and Rowe, M. 1978 Moving up: role models, mentors and the patron system. *Sloan Management Review*, **19**, 51–8.

Shaw, M.E. 1981 *Group Dynamics: The Psychology of Small Group Behaviour*. McGraw Hill, New York.

Simon, S.B., Howe, L.W. and Kirschenbaum, H. 1978 *Values Clarification: Revised Edition*. A and W Visual Library, New York.

Skevington, S. (ed) 1984 *Understanding Nurses: The Social Psychology of Nursing*. Wiley, Chichester.

Smith, S. and Smith, C. 1990 *Personal Health Choices*. Jones and Bartlett, London.

Smith, E. and Wilks, N. 1988 *Meditation*. Macdonald and Co, London.

Speizer, J.J. 1981 Role models, mentors and sponsors: the elusive concept. *Signs*, **6**, 692–712.

Stanfield, P. 1990 *Introduction to Health Professions*, 2nd edn. Jones and Bartlett, London.

Stevens, J.O. 1971 *Awareness: Exploring, Experimenting, Experiencing*. Real People Press, Moab, Utah.

Strauss, A. 1978 *Negotiations: Varieties, Contexts and Social Order*. Jossey Bass, San Francisco, California.

Sudman, S. and Bradburn, N.M. 1982 *Asking Questions: A Practical Guide to Questionnaire Design*. Jossey Bass, San Francisco, California.

Sweeney, M.A. 1985 *The Nurse's Guide to Computers*. Macmillan, New York.

Tanner, D. 1986 *That's Not What I Meant!: How Conversational Style Makes or Breaks Your Relations With Others*. Dent, London.

Taubman, B. 1976 *How to Become an Assertive Woman*. Simon and Schuster, New York.

Taylor, S. 1986 Mentors: Who are they and what are they doing? *Thrust For Educational Leadership*, **15 (7)**, 39–41.

Taylor, E. 1988 Anger intervention. *American Journal of Occupational Therapy*, **42 (3)**, 147–55.

Thygerson, A. 1989 *Fitness and Health: Lifestyle Strategies*. Jones and Bartlett, London.

Torrington, D. 1982 *Face-To-Face in Management*. Prentice Hall, Englewood Cliffs, New Jersey.

Totton, N. and Edmonston, E. 1988 *Reichian Growth Work: Melting the Blocks to Life and*

Love. Prism Press, Bridport.

Tough, A.M. 1982 *Intentional Changes: A Fresh Approach to Helping People Change*. Cambridge Books, New York.

Trower, P. (ed) 1984 *Radical Approaches to Social Skills Training*. Croom Helm, London.

Trower, P., Bryant, B.M. and Argyle, M. (eds) 1981 *Social Skills and Mental Health*. Methuen, London.

Trower, P., O'Mahony, J.M. and Dryden, W. 1982. Cognitive aspects of social failure: some implications for social skills training: *British Journal of Guidance and Counselling*, **10**, 176–84.

Truax, C.B. and Carkuff, R.R. 1967 *Towards Effective Counselling and Psychotherapy*. Aldine, Chicago.

Tschudin, V. 1986 *Counselling Skills for Nurses*. Balliere Tindall, London.

Tschudin, V. and Schober, J. 1990 *Managing Yourself*. Macmillan, London.

Wallace, W.A. 1986 *Theories of Counselling and Psychotherapy: A Basic Issues Approach*. Allyn and Bacon, Boston.

Wallis, R. 1984 *Elementary Forms of the New Religious Life*. Routledge and Kegan Paul, London.

Watkins, J. 1978 *The Therapeutic Self*. Human Science Press, New York.

Wheeler, D.D. and Janis, I.L. 1980 *A Practical Guide for Making Decisions*. Free Press, New York.

Whitaker, D.S. 1985 *Using Groups to Help People*. Tavistock/Routledge, London.

Wilkinson, J. and Canter, S. 1982 *Social Skills Training Manual: Assessment, Programme Design and Management of Training*. Wiley, Chichester.

Wlodkowski, R.J. 1985 *Enhancing Adult Motivation to Learn*. Jossey Bass, San Francisco, California.

Woodward, J. 1988 *Understanding Ourselves: The Uses of Therapy*. Macmillan, London.

Zander, A. 1982 *Making Groups Effective*. Jossey Bass, San Francisco.

Index